BARCELONA
ENCOUNTER

DAMIEN SIMONIS

Barcelona Encounter
1st edition – May 2007

Published by Lonely Planet Publications Pty Ltd
ABN 36 005 607 983

Australia Head Office, Locked Bag 1, Footscray, Vic 3011
☎ 03 8379 8000 fax 03 8379 8111
talk2us@lonelyplanet.com.au

USA 150 Linden St, Oakland, CA 94607
☎ 510 893 8555
toll free 800 275 8555
fax 510 893 8572
info@lonelyplanet.com

UK 72–82 Rosebery Ave,
Clerkenwell, London EC1R 4RW
☎ 020 7841 9000 fax 020 7841 9001
go@lonelyplanet.co.uk

This title was commissioned in Lonely Planet's London office and produced by: **Commissioning Editors** Sally Schafer, Korina Miller **Coordinating Editors** Adrienne Costanzo, Yvonne Byron **Coordinating Cartographer** Kusnandar **Layout Designer** Evelyn Yee **Managing Editor** Bruce Evans **Senior Editor** Katie Lynch **Managing Cartographer** Mark Griffiths **Cover Designer** Pepi Bluck **Project Manager** Chris Love **Series Designers** Nic Lehman, Wendy Wright **Thanks to** Amanda Canning, Rebecca Dandens, Sally Darmody, Quentin Frayne, Laura Jane, Craig Kilburn, Stephanie Pearson, Paul Piaia, Celia Wood

Photographs by Guy Moberly/Lonely Planet Images except for the following: p6, p35 Advanced Music; p 59, p82, p108, p140 Damien Simonis; p33, p34, p36 Turisme de Catalunya. **Cover photograph** La Confiteria bar, Massimo Borchi/Atlantide.

ISBN 978 1 74059 701 2

Printed through Colorcraft Ltd, Hong Kong.
Printed in China

Acknowledgement Barcelona Metro Map © TMB 2006.

HOW TO USE THIS BOOK

Colour-Coding & Maps

Colour-coding is used for symbols on maps and in the text that they relate to (eg all eating venues on the maps and in the text are given a green fork symbol). Each neighbourhood also gets its own colour, and this is used down the edge of the page and throughout that neighbourhood section.

Shaded yellow areas on the maps are to denote 'areas of interest' – be that for historical significance, attractive architecture or a strip that's good for bars or restaurants. We'd encourage you to head to these areas and just start exploring!

Prices

Multiple prices listed with the reviews (eg €10/5 or €10/5/20) indicate adult/child, adult/concession or adult/child/family.

Send us your Feedback | We love to hear from readers – your comments help make our books better. We read every word you send us, and we always guarantee that your feedback goes straight to the appropriate authors. The most useful submissions are rewarded with a free book. To send us your updates and find out about Lonely Planet events, newsletters and travel news – visit our award-winning website: ***lonelyplanet.com/contact***.

Note: We may edit, reproduce and incorporate your comments in Lonely Planet products such as guidebooks, websites and digital products, so let us know if you don't want your comments reproduced or your name acknowledged. For a copy of our privacy policy visit ***lonelyplanet.com/privacy***.

DAMIEN SIMONIS

Damien occasionally steps onto the minuscule balcony that juts out from his Eixample flat and wonders by what stroke of luck he wound up in this seaside haven. He has been in and out for years, watching Barcelona grow into one of Europe's most popular cities. It all started on a visit prior to the 1992 Olympics. Something hooked him that hasn't let go. He still finds it remarkable that in so small a space a city manages to cram in such variety and life. For Damien's money, Barcelona is as close as possible to an urban paradise on earth.

DAMIEN'S THANKS

Many in Barcelona make working here a pleasure. They include Edith López García, María Barbosa Pérez (and Enric), Susan Kempster, Michael van Laake and Rocio Vázquez, Susana Pellicer, Ottobrina Voccoli, Peter Sotirakis, Teresa Moreno Quintana and Carlos Sanagus, Sandra Candas, Nicole Neuefeind, Armin Teichmann & Co, José María Toro, Simona Volonterio, Oscar Elias, Ralf Himburg and Lilian Müller, Steven Muller and Veronika Brinkmann, Sarah Allibone, Brian and Marta O'Hare, Anna Arcarons, Alfredo López, Núria Vilches and John Rochlin (and ASBA).

THE PHOTOGRAPHER

Guy Moberly left London and a thriving photographic career for Barcelona just over seven years ago after winning *El Pais'* reportage award for a photographic series on Bulgarian orphanages. He loves the Mediterranean climate and, above all, the light. He claims Spanish *festas* to be among the best (and most unruly) in the world; *el correfoc de la Bisbal* is his favourite. Barcelona has fuelled Guy's passion for cooking: picking fresh figs every year and making compote, and every November/December diving for sea urchins then eating them on the beach.

Escribà patisserie on La Rambla (p55)

CONTENTS

THIS IS BARCELONA

A compact seaside metropolis, Barcelona is a bright, fiery star lapped by the Mediterranean, a magnet to everyone from art-loving beach bums to business execs with a weakness for sunny downtime. Immigrants from Europe, Africa, South America and Asia are stirring new colours into the already potent mix. Barcelona is a bicultural city at heart, with two languages (Catalan and Spanish) and a population whose forebears come from all over Spain.

Barcelona marries past with future in a present that seems in constant motion. At its core lies one of Europe's best preserved Gothic-era city centres. Gaudí and the Modernistas left a zany splash of weird and wonderful buildings around the city, and the same adventurousness rules today, as international architects unleash the full arsenal of their fantasy. As skyline symbols, Gaudí's Sagrada Família now has stiff competition in Jean Nouvel's shimmering, polychrome cucumber, the Torre Agbar. World-class museums take you from giant Romanesque frescoes to the playfulness of Joan Miró, from pre-Columbian South American gold to early Picasso.

The city bristles with architectural and artistic treasures but some locals prefer to practise their own talents, like the skate-boarders in the square outside the Macba contemporary art museum. It seems the entire city is always out to lunch and dinner, offering an incredible palette for the palate, from traditional Catalan cooking to 21st-century *nueva cocina española* (new Spanish cuisine) kookiness. A plethora of tippling establishments and dance clubs spreads in a hedonistic arc across the city. Countless one-off boutique shops compete with worldwide name stores. Barcelona is an intoxicating ride. Once is unlikely to be enough.

Top left Drinking at Plaça Reial (p52) **Bottom** Sónar festival (p35)

>HIGHLIGHTS

Camp Nou Stadium, home to FC Barcelona

>1 LA SAGRADA FAMÍLIA

SCALING THE DIZZY HEIGHTS OF LA SAGRADA FAMÍLIA

It is Spain's most visited sight – and the blinking thing isn't even finished! For many, that is part of the attraction. If you have been to Barcelona before, you have probably already visited Antoni Gaudí's La Sagrada Família church (p109). But that was last time, wasn't it? A work in progress, it is never quite the same. To enter La Sagrada Família is to crawl around inside one of the 20th century's most eccentric architectural minds.

Gaudí planned three façades, dedicated to the Nativity (largely done in Gaudí's lifetime), the Passion and the Glory; the latter is the main one, on which work is now under way. Each is to be crowned by four towers, representing the 12 apostles. Four higher towers will symbolise the Evangelists, while a colossal 170m-high central tower, flanked by another bearing a statue of the Virgin, will represent the Lord.

There are two ways to experience the majesty of this divine construction site. First, by looking upwards. The Nativity façade tells the story of Christ's birth and also represents the virtues of Faith, Hope and Charity. Local plant species and the nearby Montserrat mountain range inspired much of the curvaceous sculpture. The Passion façade invites you to look skyward, following the story of Christ's passion and death. Inside the five-nave interior, you cannot fail to follow the sinewy lines of the forest of treelike pillars upwards, where they splay outwards in a canopy of concrete branches to hold up the recently completed roof.

Then you can do the opposite. Lifts and stairs allow you to ascend a tower of each façade and so look down over the splendid work below, the city around and perhaps feel a breath of the heavenly inspiration that touched Gaudí.

BIRD'S-EYE VIEWS

More than two million visitors a year don't seem to bother the pair of peregrine falcons that nests high up in one of the Sagrada Família's towers. The last of these majestic birds living in Barcelona had been killed in 1973 but, since 1999, four pairs have been reintroduced, including this one with the rather exclusive address.

Get here as early in the morning as you can to avoid the worst of the crowds. Photography fans might want to catch the early sunlight on the exterior and turn up before opening time. An alternative is seeing it lit up at night (lights are usually out by midnight).

>2 CARRER DE MONTCADA

STROLLING DOWN MEDIEVAL CARRER DE MONTCADA

You'll know you're in what was once one of the wealthiest streets in medieval Barcelona when you see the queues outside the centuries-old mansions that constitute the Museu Picasso (pictured right).

In the 12th century, when Barcelona emerged as one of the main Mediterranean trading hubs, Carrer de Montcada was laid out to connect the then waterfront with one of the main roads from the city to Rome. The street became one of the snootiest addresses in town.

Looking south, the first five mansions in a row on the left now house the Museu Picasso (p79). The first three, Palau Aguilar (No 15), Palau del Baró de Castellet (No 17) and Palau Meca (No 19), all date from the 13th and 14th centuries and are home to the permanent collection. The 18th-century Casa Mauri (No 21), built over medieval remains (even some Roman leftovers have been identified), and the 14th-century Palau Finestres (No 23) accommodate temporary exhibitions.

All these hefty stone mansions are built around charming courtyards. External staircases wind up to the main, or noble, floor, where the owners would hold banquets.

No desire to queue for Picasso's early works? Head across the road! Two more fine medieval mansions house, respectively, the Museu Barbier-Mueller d'Art Precolombí (p75) and Museu Tèxtil i d'Indumentària (p79). The courtyard café-restaurant in the latter is delightful and the pre-Columbian gold and jewellery in the former a treat. Several other houses are commercial art galleries. The biggest is the 16th-century Palau dels Cervelló (No 25), home to the Paris-based Galeria Maeght. Try to peek into the baroque courtyard of Palau de Dalmases (No 20, p87), now a fanciful place to sip wine by candlelight.

PICASSO IN BARCELONA

Málaga-born Pablo Ruiz Picasso (1881–1973) arrived in Barcelona just before his 14th birthday in 1895. He studied at art school in La Llotja, in La Ribera, and later led a Bohemian lifestyle with fellow artists in various louche districts of the city. But the bright lights of Paris were too tempting and in 1904 he left Barcelona for good.

>3 MUSEU NACIONAL D'ART DE CATALUNYA

MARVELLING AT CATALUNYA'S ARTISTIC HERITAGE IN THE MUSEU NACIONAL D'ART DE CATALUNYA (MNAC)

As many Catalans will tell you, Catalonia is not Spain, but a nation with its own proud history. The collections inside the grand Palau Nacional (National Palace) are a worthy calling card for any country. The palace was raised in 1926–29 as a magnificent, if temporary, pavilion for the 1929 World Exhibition.

There is nothing temporary about it today. The Museu Nacional d'Art de Catalunya (p148) is a one-stop immersion course on the world of (mostly) Catalan art, from medieval church frescoes to chairs designed by Gaudí. The highlight is the Romanesque art collection.

In the 1920s, art historians combed hundreds of churches dotting the northern Catalan countryside. Inside they uncovered an unprecedented treasure: remains of bright Romanesque frescoes, some dating back to the 11th and 12th centuries. To save them from further decay, many were removed to Barcelona. Today, we can admire them in the re-created interiors of those churches. The most striking frescoes are those of Mary and the Christ Child (Room 7), taken from the church of Santa Maria de Taüll in Catalonia's northwest, and the majestic depiction of Christ (Room 5) from the nearby church of Sant Climent. Frescoes, carvings and altar frontals complement the collection.

The Gothic art that follows is a broad-ranging mix covering key Catalans such as Bernat Martorell and Jaume Huguet, and art from their contemporaries across Spain. Another highlight is the Thyssen-Bornemisza collection, with an eclectic range including works by Venetian Renaissance masters Veronese, Titian and Canaletto.

Catalan artists of the realist, Modernista (Catalan Art Nouveau; including Ramón Casas and Santiago Rusiñol) and Noucentista (early-20th-century) movements are then featured. Watch out for the comprehensive coin collection, which runs from Roman days to the present, and fascinating photo gallery, with extensive black-and-white archives from the best of Catalan snappers. After this, you'll be grateful for the museum's restaurant!

ALWAYS LOOK ON THE BRIGHT SIDE

One Romanesque altar frontal (Room 10) depicts saints being boiled, having nails slammed into their heads and – always a crowd pleaser – being sawn in half from head to toe. In such images the saints always appear remarkably calm, a lesson to the brethren of the ultimate righteousness of those who die for the faith…but a hard act to follow!

>4 ESGLÉSIA DE SANTA MARIA DEL MAR

MEDITATING ON TIMES PAST IN THE ESGLÉSIA DE SANTA MARIA DEL MAR

In 1384, the grand, bare Gothic church of Our Lady of the Sea (p75) was blessed. Standing before its sober entrance, flanked by two stout octagonal towers, we sense that this is quite unlike other European churches.

It is not just that this is one of the purest examples of Catalan Gothic, generously broad and bereft of the baubles that characterise the Gothic temples of other climes. It was raised in record time, a mere 59 years. With all the technology and equipment available today, Mr Gaudí's La Sagrada Família church has taken longer and still isn't finished.

This soaring temple is remarkable for its architectural harmony. While many European churches portray several styles because they took so long to build, Santa Maria del Mar benefited aesthetically from the haste of its construction. Inside, the main body is made up of a central nave and two flanking aisles separated by slender octagonal pillars, creating a sense of enormous lateral space and serenity – a great place for some quiet meditation. While the acoustics aren't great, but this is often the setting for concerts.

Typically for the times, the church was raised around its Romanesque predecessor (itself on the site of an ancient Roman cemetery), which was progressively dismantled as work advanced. Santa Maria del Mar has had some rocky moments. Work halted for years

THE PEOPLE'S CHURCH

Imagine the religious devotion of the city's porters, who spent a day each week carrying on their backs the stone required to build the church from royal quarries in Montjuïc! Their very blood is etched into the church's walls. Their memory lives on in reliefs of them in the main doors and stone carvings elsewhere in the church. Those who read Spanish should grab Ildefonso Falcones' *La Catedral del Mar* (Church of the Sea), which tells this fascinating story.

after the plague of 1348 decimated the population of the city. An earthquake in 1373 and fire six years later damaged the unfinished building. Much later, anarchists gutted it in 1909 and 1936.

Opposite its southern flank, an eternal flame burns over a sunken square. This was El Fossar de les Moreres (the Mulberry Cemetery), where Catalan resistance fighters were buried after the siege of Barcelona ended in defeat in September 1714.

>5 LA RAMBLA

TAKING THE CITY'S PULSE FROM LA RAMBLA, ITS BUSIEST BOULEVARD

Perhaps the best time to wander down La Rambla is dawn on a crisp sunny day. The street cleaners have been through, the revellers are tucked up in bed and everything is strangely quiet.

By day and night, multitudes stream along this tree-lined pedestrian boulevard (flanked by two clogged traffic lanes), a stage for street performers (from flamenco dancers to fire-eaters and more human statues than you could knock over in one go), pickpockets, three-cups-and-a-ball tricksters and more. Rip-off pavement cafés, Australian pubs, and newsstands bursting with porn add to local colour, although Barcelonins are largely noticeable by their absence.

As day turns to night, street-walkers of all persuasions come out to play and many out-of-towners become more vocal as they revel into the wee hours.

La Rambla gets its name from a seasonal stream (*raml* in Arabic) that ran here. By medieval times it was known as the Cagalell (from *caga*, shit). This open-air sewer was filled in by the 18th century. La

Rambla changes name five times along its 1.25km and if you can take your eyes off the human spectacle, there is plenty to see from Plaça de Catalunya to the Monument a Colom (p92).

Just north of Carrer del Carme, the Església de Betlem (p48) is one of the few baroque churches in Barcelona. Next up is the rococo Palau de la Virreina (p190), while on the other side of La Rambla, Palau Moja is a rare example of the neoclassical. It houses the regional government bookshop and exhibition space. To the south, Plaça de la Boqueria is marked by a Miró pavement mosaic and the nearby Mercat de la Boqueria (p56).

Aside from the market, one thing that does attract Barcelona folks to La Rambla is the Gran Teatre del Liceu (p49) opera house. Further on, you could pop into the Museu de Cera (p50), the wax museum.

ALL A-TWITTER

For more than 150 years, little birds and animals have been sold by 11 *ocellaires* (bird-keepers) on La Rambla. These stands are fighting for the right to stay, as their presence contravenes new city rules on cruelty to animals.

>6 PARK GÜELL

FALLING UNDER A SPELL IN PARK GÜELL

What a fine flop! What started as the dream of a Barcelona magnate for an English-style 'garden city' for the hoity-toity ended up as an enchanting public space, Park Güell (p128). Turn up at the main entrance on Carrer d'Olot, and you'll feel you're entering Alice's Wonderland. Key to a romantic stroll is arriving at opening time, preferably midweek.

In 1900 Eusebi Güell set his favourite architect, Antoni Gaudí, to work on what he thought would be a money-spinner. Five years earlier he had bought 15 hectares of rough land, which he planned to convert into 60 blocks for Barcelona's rich. By 1914 he had given up, with only three blocks sold, but not before Gaudí had created 3km of roads and walks, a plaza and two gatehouses.

Back to the gates. Two gingerbread houses of soft brown stone, topped by curvaceous, creamy-looking roofs decorated in *trencadís* (broken up ceramics) greet you upon entry. The one on the right, the former porter's lodge, houses the Centre d'Interpretació in the Pavelló de Consergeria, with a display on Gaudí's building methods and the history of the park.

Slip by the masses taking snaps of the ceramic decorated lizard on the stairs, now one of the city's icons, to the great pillared hall above, the Sala Hipóstila, which would have housed the garden city's market. Its roof is a grand viewing platform across the city, lined by the Banc de Trencadís, a delightful bench that snakes around its perimeter and clad with candy-coloured ceramics. The spired, pink hued house to the right is the Casa Museu Gaudí, where Gaudí lived for most of his last 20 years (1906–26).

Stroll along the 3km of sculpted paths and porticos in search of more splendid city views. You may spot residents sunning themselves on the terrace of the only extant private mansion, Casa Trias, built on the other two blocks Güell managed to flog.

GAUDÍ'S RIGHT-HAND MAN

When young architect Josep Maria Jujol (1879–1949) met Antoni Gaudí, they got along famously and, by 1904, Jujol was working with the genius. In Park Güell, his biggest contribution was the Banc del Trencadis, finished in 1906, the same year he received his architecture degree.

>7 FC BARCELONA

SITTING ON THE EDGE OF YOUR SEAT AT A BARÇA MATCH

For the sport-minded, little can match the glory and spectacle of a football match at FC Barcelona's Camp Nou stadium – one of the biggest and best in the world (and scheduled to be expanded in coming years). The athletic genius of players such as Brazil's Ronaldinho and local boy Carles Puyol is enough to have you sitting on the edge of your seat – you, along with 100,000 other spectators when the stadium fills for big clashes like the derby with arch-rivals Real Madrid.

The stadium is imposing. On key match days, people can be seen streaming towards it from all directions hours before kick-off. When they play at night, you may well notice a string of transsexual hookers in the streets around the stadium. This is their traditional patch, game or no game. By the ticket windows a squad of ticket scalpers operates more or less discreetly.

Once inside, the sheer size of the stadium becomes evident. Although not the rowdiest supporters, local fans are ardent about their team and the atmosphere can be electric. For many, FC Barcelona (known as Barça by the aficionados) is the embodiment of the Catalan spirit. Founded in 1899, it is one of Europe's biggest (and wealthiest) clubs and has been in the top ranks of Spanish football from the beginning.

If you can't manage to see a match, the Museu del Futbol Club de Barcelona (p136) will provide some consolation (and a view of the stadium). It's often as crowded as the 6yd box for a corner. On

BUMS ON SEATS

New members have flocked to FC Barcelona in recent years, with total membership rising from 106,000 in 2003 to 140,000 in mid-2006. Known as *culés* (a curious name derived from 'cul', or bottom, supposedly in reference to bottoms you could once see balancing on the outer walls of the team's one-time stadium in the district of Les Corts), some 70% of these diehard fans reside in Catalonia, but you'll find *culés* far and wide, from London to Tokyo.

display are stacks of photographs, mementos, models, sculptures, posters, programmes, jerseys, boots and balls. You can join a guided tour that takes in such delights as the players' dressing rooms, sans players. You can even relive the excitement by watching videos of goals scored.

>8 MUSEU MARÍTIM

MUSING ON EPIC SEAFARING AT THE MUSEU MARÍTIM

Climb aboard the life-size replica of the Don Juan of Austria's elaborately adorned 16th-century galley. Try to imagine (with the aid of a clever audiovisual simulation) what life was like aboard this warship. Hundreds of men chained in rows to the giant oars that drove this vessel along at up to nine knots. The cracking of whips, the agony of this mix of slaves, prisoners and desperate volunteers. The sheer stench. These wretches ate, slept and went to the toilet where they sat. They say you could *smell* a medieval galley from miles away.

Don Juan's galley was made and launched here, at the Reials Drassanes (Royal Shipyards) and sailed to lead the Spanish contingent in the last great sea battle using such vessels. This was at the Battle of Lepanto in 1571, fought between a Spanish-Venetian alliance and the Turks. The latter lost but the Europeans failed to press home the advantage.

The shipyards were completed in 1378 and are a superb example of civic Catalan Gothic architecture. Barcelona was at that period in history a major player in Mediterranean commerce, with territories and entrepôts spread across its length and breadth. As many as 30 galleys could be built beneath the shipyards' lofty arches at any one time and then slipped directly into the Mediterranean, which lapped the buildings' seaward side until the 18th century. By then, there was no longer any need to build ships here, and the yards were neglected until the 1940s, when the Museu Marítim (p93) was first located on the site. The museum is one of the most fascinating in the city.

Among the extensive collection of maritime paraphernalia on display at the museum are vessels and models of all types and representing all epochs, from coastal fishing skips to giants of the steam age. Models of the vessels Columbus led on his first voyage of accidental discovery of the Americas in 1492 are on show, along with intriguing copies of medieval atlases and navigation charts. Life-size dioramas and audiovisuals help re-create the scene of 19th century Barcelona's docklands, in their heyday among the greatest in Europe.

Outside and partly obscured by rampant vegetation along the Avinguda del Paral.lel side of the building are the most significant remnants of the city walls, which were erected here in the 13th century and later extended under count-king Pere el Ceremoniós (1336–87).

>9 MONTJUÏC

WANDERING THE FRAGRANT GARDENS OF MONTJUÏC

Barcelona is one of the noisier cities in Europe, and there's no better antidote to the grinding decibel assault of traffic, roadworks, sirens and blaring music than a lazy day of strolling amid the beauty and serenity of soothing gardens, all the while gazing back on the urban madness below?

A trip to Montjuïc is already a must for its many fine museums, led by the Museu Nacional d'Art de Catalunya (MNAC; p148) and Fundació Joan Miró (p143), but it's also worth coming here just for a wander.

Start at the Museu Militar in Castell de Montjuïc (p148; gardens pictured right). Below its sandy walls, a walking path offers views over the wide blue sea. Follow it downhill (beside Carrer de Montjuïc) from the fort and you arrive at the Jardins del Mirador, a good look-out point where a couple of snack bars await.

About 100m further on you reach the Jardins de Joan Brossa (p146). It is hard to believe there was once an amusement park in this delicately landscaped set of gardens bursting with Mediterranean flora, including cypresses, various species of pine and the occasional palm. Kids can hit the swings.

Making your way west through the gardens, you exit at Carrer Baix del Castell. Across the road, the Jardins de Mossèn Cinto de Verdaguer (p146) open up. These gentle, emerald sloping gardens are devoted to bulbs (tulips, dahlias, crocuses and more) and delicate water plants, such as lotus, water lilies and irises. There is no better spot in Barcelona for a snooze under a tree.

GETTING AROUND MONTJUÏC

In addition to the PM public bus line, which covers much of Montjuïc, a hop-on hop-off service, the Bus Montjuïc Turístic (adult/child €3/2) operates two interlocking circuits daily from the end of June to mid-September. The blue circuit starts at Plaça d'Espanya and the red line at Plaça del Portal de la Pau, at the port end of La Rambla.

Heading down Avinguda de Miramar towards the port, the Jardins de Mossèn Costa i Llobera (p146) make for a final floral fling. The thundering traffic below robs this place of tranquillity but the tropical and desert plants – including a veritable forest of cacti – are worth a look.

>10 EL RAVAL

REVELLING IN EL RAVAL

Of the old town districts, El Raval (p65) is the grittiest and perhaps the sexiest. Long a slum and still edgy in parts, it is perfect for long nights crawling the bars. The choice is ample, from taverns with a century's history to cool new bars, from dives to a couple of the city's most popular clubs. The punters are as varied. Local students compete with international stag-night groups for elbow room at the bar.

Approach it from any angle. Just off the lower end of La Rambla is a classic little, and we mean little, bar known for its dedication to *la chanson française* (French cabaret songs), Bar Pastís (p71). A short hop around the corner, through the crowds of mostly foreign punters, Kentucky (p72) was once a US Navy sailors' haunt in the depths of the then red-light district. Today, this bar attracts local bohemians and out-of-towners. A few steps back towards La Rambla, Moog (p73) is a popular dance den. A block north, the Modernista London Bar (p73) has been drawing tipplers for a century, while Bar Marsella (p70), up on Carrer de Sant Pau, has been serving absinthe in surroundings largely untouched since the early 19th century. As you wander towards it along Carrer de Sant Ramon, note the prostitutes, pimps and petty hash dealers.

Veering left, you emerge onto Rambla del Raval, a broad, mostly pedestrian boulevard that hosts a series of kebab joints and several bars, such as the funky, dark Zentraus (p73). The street's public benches are to a great extent occupied by chatting Pakistani residents. Stop in at Casa Almirall (p72), another historic watering hole and one of several student bars lining Carrer de Joaquím Costa, before winding up at one of the city's most eclectic clubs, the one-time concert hall of La Paloma (p73; pictured right).

CRACKING DOWN ON NIGHT OWLS

The constabulary have finally heeded residents' calls for quiet. Classic bars like London Bar and Kentucky, long loved for their extended hours (to 5am), have been told to shut the doors by 3am, like everyone else.

NEW

>11 LA BOQUERIA

TAKING A BITE OF MARKET LIFE IN LA BOQUERIA

One can only agree with the decision in the 19th century to replace the St Joseph monastery with the Mercat de Sant Josep, better known as La Boqueria (p56). This temple of temptation is one of Europe's greatest permanent produce fairs.

Restaurant chefs scour the *parades* (stands) in search of ingredients for the day's menus. Swarms of locals come to stock their pantries, increasingly accompanied by bands of tourists. It's no easy task getting past the gawping tour groups to buy that tempting piece of Asturian *queso de cabra* (goat's cheese). Come in the morning to avoid the crowds.

Enter from La Rambla and you are plunged into a cornucopia of fruit, vegetables and all sorts of fancy candied sweets, nuts and more on the right. To the left you'll find cheeses and all sorts of sausages, *jamón* (cured ham) and other cold meats from all over the country, along with butchers' stands.

Maintain a direct course into the elliptical heart of the market and you arrive at the Illa del Peix (the Fish Block), a series of stands creaking beneath the weight of tonnes of fresh, glistening seafood of every possible description. Apart from classics such as flat grey *lenguado* (sole) to great chunks of *pez espada* (swordfish), you'll notice the prized burnt-red *gambes de Palamòs*, netted off the Costa Brava and among the tastiest prawns on offer in Barcelona's better restaurants. Some fine wine shops shelter beneath the pillars of a portico on the market's northern flank.

At lunchtime, market workers and interlopers jostle for a stool at several bars in the market, among the better of which are Bar Pinotxo and Bar Central. It's a great chance to sample the market's produce.

Late at night, the poorly lit passages between tightly shut stands become the arena of a handful of mostly transsexual sex workers going about their business with impromptu clients fished in off La Rambla.

TASTE TWINS

Barcelona's La Boqueria and London's Borough market (the grand-daddy of the two, with 250 years of history, although a junior in terms of size) signed a symbolic twinning agreement in April 2006. The markets' avowed aim is to promote their respective images and encourage the consumption of quality fresh produce.

>12 TIBIDABO

CATCHING THE TIBIDABO TRAM & SOME WILD RIDES

Come to the mountain. An old-style family outing, the trip out to the city's highest peak, Tibidabo (512m), bursts with nostalgia. The panoramic vistas are themselves a fine reward; timeless amusement park rides (pictured above) are a retro trip to fun parks of yore.

Barcelona has rediscovered the tram and installed a couple of lines serving the 'burbs. But one rattler from the good ol' days never stopped. An old charmer, the Tramvia Blau (Blue Tram) starts at Plaça de John F Kennedy and clunks its way 1.3km up Avinguda del Tibidabo to the funicular station at the amusement park. Virtually nothing has changed since the line opened in October 1901. From the polished timber seats admire the fine mansions as you chug along. The single-wagon tram runs weekends and holidays (from 10am until at least 6pm) all year, and daily late June to early September.

The rattling ascent continues with the Funicular, which whisks you to the top of the mountain, from where you can see the whole city. For still better views (and often a chill wind), head inside the Temple del Sagrat Cor and take the lift to the roof. The church, started in 1902 and only completed in 1961, is reminiscent of Paris' Sacré-Cœur church in Montmartre and equally prominent. You can see miles out to sea and inland as far as the weird-looking Montserrat mountain range. For more views take the lift to the top of the Torre de Collserola (p137), a telecommunications tower designed by Sir Norman Foster.

The kids will be dragging you along to Parc d'Atraccions (p136), Barcelona's old-style fun park, where one of the star attractions is the Krueger Hotel, a nerve-rattling house of horrors.

>BARCELONA DIARY

Naturally inclined to enjoying themselves, Barcelonins put on a crammed calendar of events to suit every taste: from the fiery madness of the traditional summer solstice Nit de Foc and September's Festes de la Mercè to theatre festivals, citywide jazz feasts and one of Europe's top electronic music get-togethers. In summer especially, districts party in the streets in a series of local *festes* (feasts) that involve bands, carousing and precious little sleep. For more, go to www.bcn.es and click on Diary in the English version of the homepage. For a list of public holidays, see p186.

Carnaval at Sitges (p34)

JANUARY

Reis/Reyes

Christmas comes later for Spanish kids, as presents are handed out for the Epifanía (Epiphany) on 6 January. The evening before, children delight in the Cavalcada dels Reis Mags (Parade of the Three Kings; pictured right), with floats, music and bucket loads of sweets chucked into the scrambling crowds.

SUMMER STAGES & LATIN HEAT

Many theatres shut down for summer, but into the breach steps the Festival del Grec (www.barcelonafestival.com) programme of theatre, dance and music, which lasts from late June until well into August. Performances are held all over the city, not just at the open-air Teatre Grec amphitheatre on Montjuïc (Map pp144–5, E3) from which the festival takes its name. For Hispanic live music, Barnasants (www.barnasants.com) is hot. The city's live-music venues host a bevy of Catalan, Spanish and Latin American singer-songwriters for concerts from late January until mid-March.

FEBRUARY

Carnestoltes/Carnaval (Carnival)

Barcelona's Carnival is colourful enough but the real fun happens in Sitges (see p110), where the gay community stages gaudy parades and party-goers let rip.

MARCH–APRIL

Divendres Sant/Viernes Santo (Good Friday)

Taste Andalucian Easter with processions from Església de Sant Agustí (Map p65, C4), featuring a float of the Virgin of the Macarena, robed members of religious fraternities and barefoot penitent women dragging crosses and chains.

Día de Sant Jordi

Catalonia celebrates St George on 23 April. Men give women a rose and women give men a book (it's also Día del Llibre, Book Day).

MAY

L'Ou Com Balla

The curious 'Dancing Egg' is an empty egg shell that bobs on top of the flower-festooned fountain in La Catedral's cloister to mark the feast of Corpus Christi (Thursday after the eighth Sunday after Easter Sunday).

Primavera Sound

www.primaverasound.com

For three days late in May and/or early June the Parc del Fòrum hosts international DJs and musicians. A winter version, Primavera Club, takes place in early December.

JUNE

Sónar

www.sonar.es

Sónar (pictured) is Barcelona's celebration of electronic music and Europe's biggest such event. See big names and experimental acts.

Día de Sant Joan/Día de San Juan Bautista (Feast of St John The Baptist)

The night before this feast day (24 June), people celebrate Berbena de Sant Joan (St John's Night), aka La Nit del Foc (Night of Fire) with drinking, dancing, bonfires and fireworks.

AUGUST

Festa Major de Gràcia

www.festamajordegracia.org

Around 15 August, this knees-up in the Gràcia area features a competition for the best-decorated street. Enjoy feasting, bands and drinking.

Festes de la Mercè

http://merce.bcn.cat

Barcelona's biggest party with *castellers, sardanes* (folk dancing), *gegants* and *capgrossos* (giants and big heads), a *correfoc* (fire race) and Barcelona Accio Musical (www.bcn.es/bam), a huge live-concert series.

REACH FOR THE SKY

Is it a sport? Is it a hobby? When there's a *festa major* (festival) on, *colles* (teams) of *castellers* ('castlers', or human castle builders; pictured above) gather in Catalonia to raise human 'castles' of at times astonishing height – up to 10 tiers. These usually involve levels of three to five people standing on each others' shoulders. A crowd of team-mates forms a supporting scrum at the base. To complete the castle, a young (and light!) child called the *anxaneta* must reach the top and wave to the crowd, the signal to start whooping with abandon and to collapse (hopefully in orderly fashion) the castle. Watch out for them in Plaça de Sant Jaume (Map p47, C3) during the Festes de la Mercè.

NOVEMBER

Festival Internacional de Jazz de Barcelona

www.the-project.net

For most of the month big venues (from l'Auditori down) host international jazz acts, such as Keith Jarrett and Barbara Hendricks in 2006. A more home-spun jazz fest also takes place in bars across the old city and many of these performances are free.

>ITINERARIES

mas
ESPATLLA
IBÈRICA
de GLA
GUIJUELO
110
mas
TENIM
TORTA
del
CASAR
mas
mas

>ITINERARIES

Barcelona has enough sights to keep you exploring for months. Luckily, the city is compact, and most spots are easy to reach on foot or by Metro. When it's time for a break, there are plenty of tempting places to get a drink and a bite to eat.

ONE DAY

A stroll along the rambunctious La Rambla (p18) is a must – duck into the Mercat de la Boqueria (p30). Once at the port, head back inland into the Barri Gòtic district. Make for Plaça de Sant Jaume and then La Catedral (p49). From here, cross Via Laietana, passing by the colourful reincarnated Mercat de Santa Caterina (p75), and veer southeast to reach the Museu Picasso (p79) and Gothic Església de Santa Maria del Mar (p16) church. Take some time out for a wine at La Vinya del Senyor (p87) and check on the offerings at the little fashion boutiques in the nearby side streets. Finish the day sampling the seafood that tempts the palate in La Barceloneta (p94).

TWO DAYS

OK, you held off on the first day, but your first stop on day two should be the magnificent Gaudí masterpiece, La Sagrada Família (p10). For a complete change of theme, head for Montjuïc. Star attractions on this hill include the Museu Nacional d'Art de Catalunya (MNAC; p14), Fundació Miró (p143), the Castell (p148) and strolls in the several gardens (p26). Snack bars abound. Wander into Poble Sec for evening gourmet snacks at Quimet I Quimet (p150) and a tipple at the unpredictable Tinta Roja (p150).

THREE DAYS

In summer you may well want some beach time. The better ones start with Platja de Nova Icària (p170), just on the northeast side of Port Olímpic. Sea dogs should visit the Museu Marítim (p24). An excursion to Gaudí's marvellous Park Güell (p21) is also a good option, for its uniqueness and the views. A meal in the Eixample area, such as at Cata 1.81 (p119), could be followed by dancing at the Sutton Club (p141).

Top Views from Castell de Montjuïc (p148) **Bottom** Prized *jamón* (cured ham) on sale **Previous Page** Fundació Joan Miró (p143)

A RAINY DAY

When it rains in Barcelona, it usually pours. Head first to the Museu d'Història de la Ciutat (p50), most of which is cosily underground and just a snap from the closest Metro stop! A quick dash gets you to the nearby Museu Frederic Marès (p51). Virtually next door is the Casa de la Pia Almoina (p48) and then La Catedral (p49). To break this up for a sustenance stop, make a run for Shunka (p60) and try some of the best Japanese fare in the city. When you're done with visiting the sights, head for Caelum (p54), a delightful shop worth browsing that doubles as a café.

Bridge to Maremàgnum shopping complex, Port Vell (p88)

FORWARD PLANNING

Opera and music lovers should think in advance. For a performance at the Gran Teatre del Liceu (p63), book on the internet as far ahead as possible. For the Palau de la Música Catalana (p87), a couple of weeks is usually enough. Motor-racing fans can combine Formula One with partying in Barcelona each April. For dates contact the Circuit de Catalunya (www.circuitcat.com) racetrack. Book tickets online for this and many events at ServiCaixa (www.servicaixa.com). FC Barcelona football fans can check the schedule for upcoming games on the club's website (www.fcbarcelona.com) but you must call to make reservations (☎ +34 93 496 36 00). Major games tend to be booked solid weeks in advance. For a fancy dinner, book a few days ahead at Saüc (p121) or Àbac (p84). The day before you head out to Barcelona, check out BCN-Nightlife (www.bcn-nightlife.com) for what's happening in the clubs.

MUSEUM MONDAYS

Many sights in the city shut on Mondays, but some buck the trend. Start with a bright art injection at the Museu d'Art Contemporani de Barcelona (Macba; p66), then wander the streets of El Raval to the Museu Marítim (p24). Now that you're all at sea, head for Port Vell. Ascend the Monument a Colom (p92), get a bite in the Maremàgnum shopping complex and proceed to l'Aquàrium (p89) for a shudder in the shark tunnel. If you're feeling energetic, make for La Ribera and cross El Born to the Parc de la Ciutadella (p80), where you could finish the day at the Zoo de Barcelona (p80).

FEELING SKINT

A busy day's sightseeing in Barcelona can be enjoyed while barely touching the wallet. A day could start at Park Güell (p21). You could continue the nature theme with a Metro and funicular ride to Montjuïc (p26) for a stroll around the gardens, which are the perfect spot for a packed picnic lunch – prepared with ingredients from La Boqueria (p30) market! Uphill, drink in the views over the Mediterranean from below the fortified walls of the Castell de Montjuïc (p148). It's free to wander into the Estadi Olímpic (p147). One of the few major museums with free entry is the delightful CaixaForum art gallery (p143), at the foot of the hill.

>NEIGHBOURHOODS

Rambla de la Raval

NEIGHBOURHOODS

Barcelona is one of the noisiest and most densely inhabited cities in Europe. The result is that the fun here comes in high-density, concentrated doses too.

At the heart is the Old City core, with 2000 years' history. Dubbed the Barri Gòtic (Gothic Quarter), it is bounded by La Rambla and Via Laietana, the former a pedestrian spectacle and the latter a boulevard of thundering traffic. In between grand churches, medieval mansions and Roman reminders, its meandering lanes are laced with old-time shops, tiny bars and charming restaurants carved out of centuries-old buildings.

Across La Rambla, El Raval is a dodgier part of the old town that teems with bars and restaurants old and new, along with the occasional street-walker and junkie. La Ribera, on the other side of Via Laietana, is home to Picasso's art, the city's greatest church and heaving nightlife along the boulevard of El Born.

Nearby, La Barceloneta is a strange mix of working-class district, sizzling fish restaurants and seemingly all of Europe's summertime youth draped along the beach. Beyond stretch more beaches past the yachties' Port Olímpic to the new district of Parc del Fòrum. Closer to the ancient heart of the city, Port Vell (Old Port) is anything but aged, with a humming modern shopping and entertainment centre and one of Europe's biggest aquariums.

Montjuïc is a hill of peace and culture, with gardens and museums. The sprawling Eixample, repository of Modernista (Catalan Art Nouveau) architecture, is divided into microzones. The gay scene, busy nightlife streets and an endless sprinkling of restaurants demand exploration. Chic shopping congregates on Passeig de Gràcia and Rambla de Catalunya.

Beyond spread the bustling, narrow streets of Gràcia and more well-to-do areas of the Zona Alta that stretch to the hills, culminating in Tibidabo.

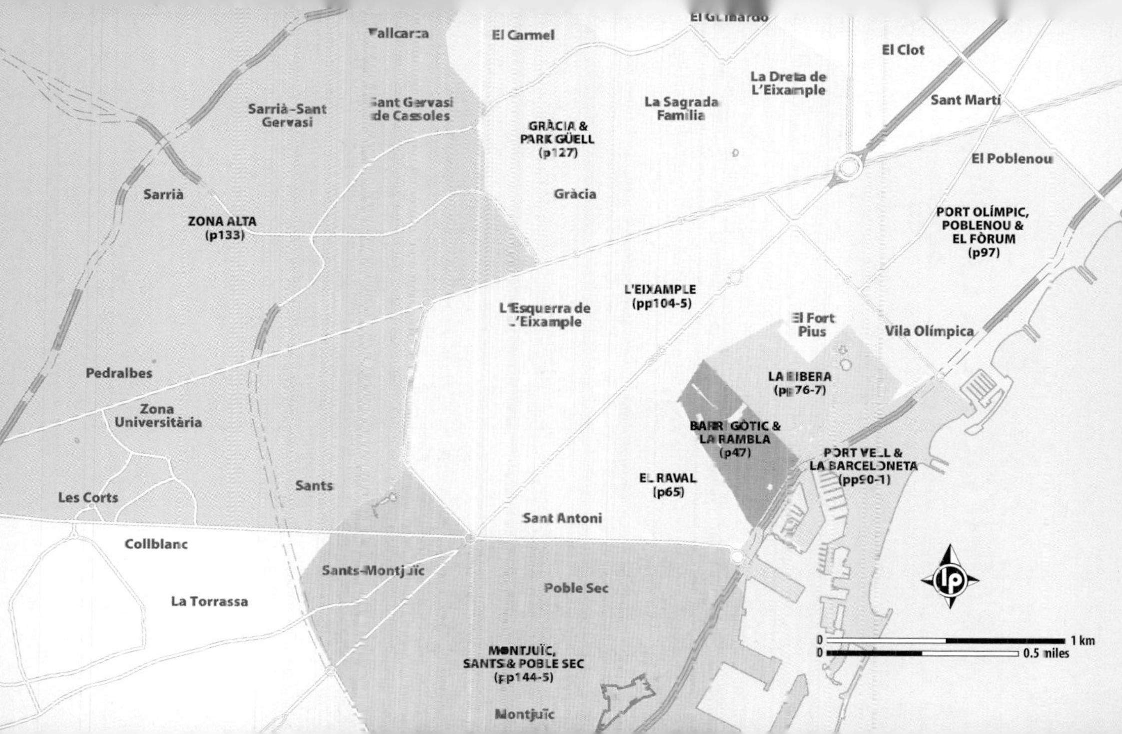

El Carmel
El Clot
La Dreta de L'Eixample
Sarrià-Sant Gervasi
La Sagrada Família
Sant Martí
GRÀCIA & PARK GÜELL (p127)
El Poblenou
Sarrià
Gràcia
ZONA ALTA (p133)
PORT OLÍMPIC, POBLENOU & EL FÒRUM (p97)
L'EIXAMPLE (pp104-5)
L'Esquerra de L'Eixample
El Fort Pius
Vila Olímpica
Pedralbes
Zona Universitària
BARRI GÒTIC & LA RAMBLA (p47)
Sants
EL RAVAL (p65)
Les Corts
Sant Antoni
Collblanc
Sants-Montjuïc
Poble Sec
La Torrassa
MONTJUÏC, SANTS & POBLE SEC (pp144-5)
Montjuïc
0
1 km
0
0.5 miles

>BARRI GÒTIC & LA RAMBLA

Everyone walks La Rambla during a Barcelona stay. Visitors outnumber locals, but that just adds to the colour. In just a 1km strip you'll find bird stalls, flower stands, buskers, bars, historic shops, grand buildings, a pungent produce market, pickpockets, prostitutes, bored police and a veritable UN of paraders. Once a sewage ditch lined by medieval walls, La Rambla marks the southwest flank of the Barri Gòtic (Gothic Quarter).

This quarter is where the Romans set up shop 2000 years ago. The city and Catalan governments reside on what was once the site of the forum. Nearby are sprinkled Gothic mansions, the cathedral, an underground slice of ancient Barcelona and leftover Roman walls. Shoppers revel along Avinguda del Portal del Àngel and Carrer de la Boqueria. Between crowded Carrer de Ferran and the port, narrow, cobbled and sometimes fetid lanes are festooned with bars and eateries.

BARRI GÒTIC & LA RAMBLA

SEE

Name	No	Grid
Ajuntament	1	C3
Casa de la Pia Almoina (Museu Diocesà)	2	C2
Casa de l'Ardiaca	3	B2
Església de Santa Anna	4	A1
Església de Santa Maria del Pi	5	B3
Església de Sants Just i Pastor	6	C3
Gran Teatre del Liceu	7	A4
La Catedral	8	C2
Museu d'Història de la Ciutat	9	C2
Museu de Cera	10	C5
Museu de l'Eròtica	11	A3
Museu del Calçat	12	B2
Museu Frederic Marès	13	C2
Palau de la Generalitat	14	C2
Palau del Lloctinent	15	C2
Plaça Reial	16	B4
Roman Cemetery	17	A2
Sinagoga Major	18	B3
Temple Romà d'Augustí	19	C2

SHOP

Name	No	Grid
Antinous	20	D5
Art Montfalcon	21	B2
Caelum	22	B2
Cereria Subirà	23	C2
Drap	24	B2
El Ingenio	25	B3
Escribà	26	A3
FC Botiga	27	D2
Ganiveteria Roca	28	A3
Gemma Povo	29	B3
Gotham	30	C3
Joguines Foyé	31	B3
La Condoneria	32	B3
Le Boudoir	33	A1
L'Herboristeria del Rei	34	B4
Mercat de la Boquiera	35	A3
Obach	36	B3
Papabubble	37	D4
Sestienda	38	B4

EAT

Name	No	Grid
Agut	39	D4
Bar Celta	40	D4
Cafè de l'Acadèmia	41	D3
Cafè de l'Òpera	42	B4
Can Culleretes	43	B4
Cometacinc	44	D3
El Paraguayo	45	D6
Los Caracoles	46	C4
Pla	47	D3
Restaurant Pitarra	48	D4
Shunka	49	B1

DRINK

Name	No	Grid
Barcelona Pipa Club	50	B4
Café Royale	51	B4
Club Rosa	52	B4
Manchester	53	D4
Milk Bar & Bistro	54	D3
Schilling	55	B4
Soul Club	56	C5
Sugar	57	B4

PLAY

Name	No	Grid
Club Fellini	58	B5
Gran Teatre del Liceu	(see 7)	
Harlem Jazz Club	59	D4
Jamboree	60	B4
New York	61	B5
Sala Tarantos	62	B4

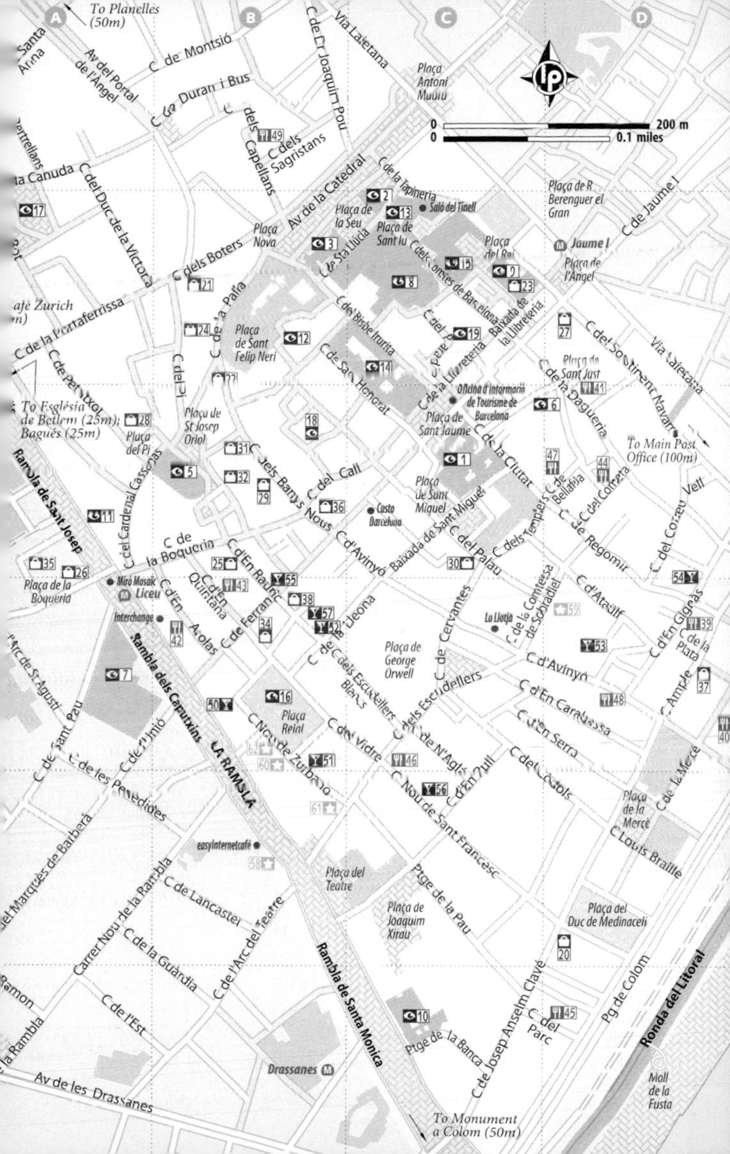
A
B
C
D
To Planelles (50m)
C de Montsió
Av del Portal de l'Àngel
C de Duran i Bus
C de Dr Joaquim Pou
Via Laietana
Plaça Antoni Maura
200 m
0.1 miles
C dels Capellans
C dels Sagristans
49
C del Duc de la Victòria
Av de la Catedral
C de la Tapineria
2
Plaça de la Seu
13
Saló del Tinell
Plaça de Sant Iu
Plaça de R Berenguer el Gran
C de Jaume I
17
Plaça Nova
3
C dels Boters
C de Sta Llúcia
C dels Comtes de Barcelona
15
Plaça del Rei
9
Jaume I
Plaça de l'Àngel
23
21
8
C de la Portaferrissa
C de la Palla
24
Plaça de Sant Felip Neri
12
C del Bisbe Irurita
C del Pi
19
Baixada de la Llibreteria
27
C del Sotsinent Navarro
Via Laietana
C de Petritxol
C de Sant Honorat
14
C de la Llibreteria
Oficina d'informació de Tourisme de Barcelona
Plaça de Sant Just
C de la Dagueria
41
To Església de Betlem (25m); Bagués (25m)
28
Plaça del Pi
Plaça de St Josep Oriol
18
Plaça de Sant Jaume
6
To Main Post Office (100m)
Rambla de Sant Josep
C del Cardenal Casañas
5
31
C dels Banys Nous
C de la Ciutat
47
44
1
32
29
C del Call
Plaça de Sant Miquel
C de Bellafila
C del Correu Vell
11
36
Casa Barcelona
Baixada de Sant Miquel
C dels Templers
C de Regomir
C de la Boqueria
C d'Avinyó
C del Palau
35
26
25
C d'En Rauric
55
30
54
Plaça de la Boqueria
Miró Mosaic
Liceu
C d'En Quintana
43
38
C de la Comtessa de Sobradiel
59
C d'Ataülf
Interchange
C de Ferran
57
52
C de Lleona
La Llotja
C de Cervantes
C d'En Gignàs
39
C de la Plata
42
C d'En Arolas
34
53
C dels Escudellers Blancs
Plaça de George Orwell
C d'Avinyó
C dels Escudellers
C Ample
37
C de l'Arc de St Agustí
7
Rambla dels Caputxins
C d'En Carabassa
48
50
16
Plaça Reial
C de Sant Pau
C de la Unió
LA RAMBLA
C Nou de Zurbano
C del Vidre
C de N'Aglà
C d'En Serra
40
62
60
51
46
C de la Mercè
C de les Penedides
56
C d'En Gual
C dels Còdols
C Nou de Sant Francesc
Plaça de la Mercè
61
C del Marquès de Barberà
C Louis Braille
easyInternetcafé
58
Plaça del Teatre
Ptge de la Pau
C de Lancaster
Carrer Nou de la Rambla
Plaça de Joaquim Xirau
Plaça del Duc de Medinaceli
C de l'Arc del Teatre
C de la Guàrdia
20
Rambla de Santa Monica
C de Josep Anselm Clavé
Pg de Colom
Ronda del Litoral
C de l'Est
10
45
C del Parc
Ptge de la Banca
Drassanes
Moll de la Fusta
Av de les Drassanes
To Monument a Colom (50m)

SEE

AJUNTAMENT

010; Plaça de Sant Jaume; 10am-1pm Sun; M Jaume I;

This town hall has been the seat of city power since the 14th century and has a Catalan Gothic side façade on Carrer de la Ciutat. Belying its blandly renovated, neoclassical front is a spectacular interior featuring a majestic staircase and the splendidly restored Saló de Cent (Chamber of the One Hundred).

CASA DE LA PIA ALMOINA (MUSEU DIOCESÀ)

93 315 22 13; www.arqbcn.org; Avinguda de la Catedral 4; adult/child under 7yr/senior & student €3/free/1.50; 10am-2pm & 5-8pm Tue-Sat, 11am-2pm Sun; M Jaume I;

Barcelona's Roman walls ran across Plaça de la Seu into what subsequently became the Casa de la Pia Almoina. This charity operated from the 11th century, but the present building dates back to the 15th century. Inside is the Museu Diocesà (Diocesan Museum), with a sparse collection of medieval religious art.

CASA DE L'ARDIACA

Carrer de Santa Llúcia 1; 9am-9pm Mon-Fri, to 2pm Sat; M Jaume I

This 16th-century house is home to the city's archives and has a supremely serene courtyard, renovated by Domènech i Montaner (p179) in 1902. You can get a good glimpse at some stout Roman walls in here.

ESGLÉSIA DE BETLEM

93 318 38 23; La Rambla dels Estudis; 9am-2pm & 6-9pm; M Liceu

The early-18th-century Church of Jerusalem was once considered the most splendid of Barcelona's few baroque offerings. Its exterior still makes a powerful impression, but arsonists destroyed much of the inside at the outset of the civil war in 1936. In the run-up to Christmas, check out the *pessebres* (nativity scenes).

ESGLÉSIA DE SANTA ANNA

93 301 35 76; Carrer de Santa Anna; 9am-1pm & 6.30-8.30pm; M Catalunya

Starting life as a Romanesque chapel in the 12th century, this tranquil house of worship is set on a square of its own. The deliciously silent and cool Gothic cloister encloses a leafy garden and fountain.

ESGLÉSIA DE SANTA MARIA DEL PI

93 318 47 43; Plaça del Pi; 8.30am-1pm & 4.30-9pm Mon-Sat, 9am-2pm & 5-9pm Sun & holidays; M Liceu

This striking church, built between 1322 and 1453, is a classic of

Catalan Gothic, with an imposing façade, a wide interior and single nave. The beautiful rose window above its entrance is thought to be the world's largest.

ESGLÉSIA DE SANTS JUST I PASTOR

93 301 74 33; Plaça de Sant Just 5; 10am-1pm & 5-8pm Mon-Sat; M Liceu/Jaume I

This single-nave church was built in 1342 in Catalan Gothic style, with chapels on either side of the buttressing. It boasts some fine stained-glass windows. On Plaça de Sant Just, in front of the church, bubbles a water fountain dating from 1367. Gaudí was arrested here one day for not speaking Spanish to a copper.

GRAN TEATRE DEL LICEU

93 485 99 00; www.liceubarcelona.com; La Rambla dels Caputxins 51-59; admission €4, guided tour adult/child under 10yr/student €6/free/4; guided tours 10am, unguided visits 11.30am, noon & 1pm; M Liceu;

Built in 1847, burned to a crisp in 1994 and resurrected five years later, this is Barcelona's grand operatic stage. It can seat up to 2300 in its auditorium, where the classic 19th-century stalls have been restored and combined with a hi-tech stage.

ROMAN WALLS

Of course, the city's first architects of note were the Romans, who built a town here in the 1st century BC. Large relics of its 3rd- and 4th-century walls can still be seen in the Barri Gòtic, particularly at Plaça de Ramon de Berenguer el Gran (D2) and by the northern end of Carrer del Sotstinent Navarro (D2).

LA CATEDRAL

93 342 82 60; Plaça de la Seu; special visit €4, other times free; 8am-12.15pm & 5.15-7.30pm, special visit 1-5pm; M Liceu/Jaume I

Barcelona's central place of worship was constructed in what was the northern half of the Roman town. The richly decorated main façade was added during the late 19th century (to a 15th-century design), while the rest of the cathedral was built between 1298 and 1460. In the middle of the central nave are the impressive 14th-century sculpted choir stalls (€1.50). Geese honk in the cloister, as they have since medieval times, and the Sala Capitular (chapter house, €1.50) boasts a handful of religious paintings. Visit the roof and tower by lift (€2) from the Capella de les Animes del Purgatori near the northeast transept. In the morning or afternoon, entrance to the cathedral is free and you can visit any combination of the choir stalls, chapter house and roof. To visit all three, it costs less (and is less crowded) if you opt for the 'special visit' between 1pm and 5pm.

MUSEU DE CERA

☎ 93 317 26 49; www.museocerabcn.com; Passatge de la Banca 7; adult/child €6.65/3.75; 10am-1.30pm & 4-7.30pm Mon-Fri, 11am-2pm & 4.30-8.30pm Sat, Sun & holidays; M Drassanes

With a collection of 300 wax figures of familiar faces from around the world, this is just as creepy as any other wax museum. More horrible than any display of twisted medieval torture are the figures of Prince Charles with Camilla.

MUSEU DE L'ERÒTICA

☎ 93 318 98 65; www.erotica-museum.com; La Rambla de Sant Josep 96; adult/senior & student €7.50/6.50; 10am-midnight Jun-Sep, 11am-9pm Oct-May; M Liceu

Falling somewhere between titillation, tawdriness and art, this private collection is devoted to sex through the ages. The décor is pseudo-seedy, and the diverse exhibits range from exquisite *Kamasutra* illustrations and Mapplethorpe photos to early porn movies, S&M apparatus and a 2m wooden penis.

MUSEU DEL CALÇAT

☎ 93 301 45 33; Plaça de Sant Felip Neri 5; admission €2.50; 11am-2pm Tue-Sun; M Liceu

This little museum of shoes is an unexpected treat: there are dainty ones, famous ones, weird ones, Roman ones, silk ones, seamless ones, baby ones and one gigantic one made for the Monument a Colom (p92).

MUSEU D'HISTÒRIA DE LA CIUTAT

☎ 93 315 11 11; www.museuhistoria.bcn.es; Carrer del Veguer; adult/student (incl Museu-Monestir de Pedralbes & Park Güell Centre de Acollida) €4/2.50, free 4-8pm 1st Sat of month, temporary exhibitions adult/student €3.50/1.50; 10am-2pm & 4-8pm Tue-Sat, 10am-3pm Sun Oct-May, 10am-8pm Tue-Sat, to 3pm Sun Jun-Sep; M Jaume I; ♿

The entrance to this museum is through the 16th-century mansion Casa Padellàs, which was shifted here, stone by stone, in the 1930s to make way for the bustling ramrod artery of Via Laietana. Digging the foundations one day, what should labourers stub their shovels on but the ancient Roman city of Barcino. Descend into the remnants of the Roman town and stroll along glass ramps above 2000-year-old streets. You walk past the old public laundries, where pots were left outside for passers-by to pee in – urine was used as a disinfectant in Roman laundries! Explore public baths and drainage systems. Peer into storage areas for wine (Catalan wine was plentiful and rough) and *garum* (a whiffy fish sauce popular throughout the Roman empire). After Barcino, you emerge into the buildings of the Palau Reial, the former royal palace, where you can admire the broad arches of the Saló del Tinell, a 14th-century banquet hall.

MUSEU FREDERIC MARÈS

☎ 93 310 58 00; www.museumares.bcn.es; Plaça de Sant Iu 5-6; adult/senior & student €3/1.50, free Wed afternoon & 1st Sun of month; 10am-7pm Tue-Sat, to 3pm Sun & holidays; M Jaume I

Within these centuries-old walls resides a mind-boggling

Museu d'Història de la Ciutat

collection of everyday items, art and medieval Spanish sculpture amassed by Frederic Marès i Deulovol (1893–1991), sculptor, traveller and hoarder extraordinaire. Have a snack in the shady courtyard café.

PALAU DE LA GENERALITAT

☎ 012; Plaça de Sant Jaume; guided tours 10am-1pm 2nd & 4th Sun of month (bring ID); M Jaume I;

This seat of Catalan government was adapted from several Gothic mansions in what had been the Jewish ghetto (known as the Call) in the early 15th century and extended over time. The original Gothic façade on Carrer del Bisbe Irurita (C2) features a relief of St George by Pere Joan in 1418.

STROLL ALONG CARRER DE LA DAGUERIA

If striding away from Plaça de Sant Jaume towards Via Laietana, stop to make a right down the delightful medieval lane of Carrer de la Dagueria (D3). In little more than 100m you'll encounter a cheese shop, a ceramics vendor, a women's bookshop and a handful of bars and places to eat. The street ends in Plaça de Sant Just, walled off to one side by the Església de Sants Just i Pastor (p49) and graced by a scattering of outdoor tables for a drink or snack.

PALAU DEL LLOCTINENT

Carrer dels Comtes de Barcelona; M Jaume I

Built in the 1550s, this palace was the residence of the *lloctinent* (Spanish viceroy) of Catalonia. It boasts a fine wooden ceiling and pleasing courtyard. Until 1993 it housed the Arxiu de la Corona d'Aragó, a unique archive documenting the history of the kingdom prior to unification under Fernando and Isabel, and may again do so from 2007.

PLAÇA REIAL

Barri Gòtic; M Liceu

This pretty 19th-century square with neoclassical façades, palm trees and numerous noisy restaurants and bars was created on the site of a convent. The elegant lampposts were Gaudí's first commission in the big smoke.

ROMAN CEMETERY

Plaça de la Vila de Madrid; M Catalunya

On a quiet square that once lay on a road leading out of Roman Barcino, this site features a series of intact Roman tombs lined up on the spot where they were found when they were excavated.

SINAGOGA MAJOR

☎ 93 317 07 90; www.calldebarcelona.org; Carrer de Marlet 5; 11am-2pm & 4-7pm Tue-Sat, 11am-2pm Sun; M Liceu

What little is left of the Jewish ghetto's main medieval synagogue was accidentally discovered in the early 2000s. In the two rooms, now again a working temple, can be seen remnants of Roman-era walls and some tanners' wells.

TEMPLE ROMÀ D'AUGUSTI

Carrer del Paradis 10; (unreliable) 10am-2pm Mon-Sat; M Jaume I

It's unremarkable from the outside, but this courtyard houses four Corinthian columns of Barcelona's main Roman temple, built in the 1st century in the name of Caesar Augustus.

SHOP

ANTINOUS *Books*

93 301 90 70; www.antinouslibros.com; Carrer de Josep Anselm Clavé 6; 11am-2pm & 5-8.30pm Mon-Fri, noon-2pm & 5-8.30pm Sat; M Drassanes

An extensive bookshop with his-and-hers gay literature, Antinous is also a centre of Bareclona's gay culture. Out the back is a relaxed café, which doubles as an exhibition space and stage for book presentations.

ART MONTFALCON *Gifts*

93 301 13 25; www.montfalcon.com; Carrer dels Boters 4; 10am-9pm; M Liceu

Beneath the overarching vaults of this Gothic cavern is spread an incredible range of gift ideas and art. The most appealing are the prints of local and universal inspiration. Thrown in are original works by local artists, framed and ready to go, and a whole range of Barcelona memorabilia, from ceramics to arty T-shirts.

BARCELONA BARGAINS

Anyone visiting from London will tell you the shopping in Barcelona is a bargain at any time of year. But serious shoppers plan their sprees around the sales (*rebaixes* in Catalan, *rebajas* in Castilian). Everything is marked down from the middle of January to the end of February, and summer styles are almost given away from around 5 July until well into August.

BAGUÉS *Jewellery*

93 318 38 42; La Rambla de Sant Josep 105; 10am-2pm & 4.30-8pm Mon-Fri, 11am-2pm Sat; M Liceu

This is more than just any old jewellery store. The boys from Bagués have been chipping away at precious stones and moulding metal since the 19th century, and many of their classic pieces have a flighty Modernista influence. There is a branch in Casa Amatller in the Manzana de la Discordia (p110).

CAELUM *Food & Drink*

☎ 93 302 69 93; Carrer de la Palla 8; 5-8.30pm Mon, 10.30am-8.30pm Tue-Thu, 10.30am-2pm Fri & Sat; M Liceu

From all corners of the country arrive the carefully prepared sweets and other goods that have been the pride of Spanish convents down the centuries. Tempting and traditional items such as sticky marzipan (made in closed-order convents) and olive oil with thyme find their way into this specialist store. Head downstairs to the cavernous café area, once a medieval Jewish bathhouse. You can also take a seat at a huddle of tables upstairs.

CERERIA SUBIRÀ *Candles*

☎ 93 315 26 06; Baixada de la Llibreteria 7; 9am-1.30pm & 4-7.30pm Mon-Fri, 9am-1.30pm Sat; M Jaume I

Even if you're not interested in flickering flames, you'll be impressed by the ornate décor here. Nobody can hold a candle to these people in terms of longevity – the Subirà name in wax and wicks has been in demand since 1761, although it's only been at this address since late in the 19th century.

DRAP *Dolls*

☎ 93 318 14 87; Carrer del Pi 14; 9.30am-1.30pm & 4.30-8.30pm Mon-Fri, 10am-1.30pm & 5-8.30pm Sat; M Liceu

This busy shop brings out the giddy little girl in all of us – which generally comes as a surprise to blokes – as it's packed to the rafters with everything relating to dolls and their well-being, from miniature jars of jam to intricate handmade mansions.

EL INGENIO *Masks*

☎ 93 317 71 38; www.el-ingenio.com; Carrer d'En Rauric 6; 10.30am-1.30pm & 4.15-8pm Mon-Fri, 11am-2pm & 5-8.30pm Sat; M Liceu

Liven up your party with El Ingenio's bewildering range of tricks, fancy dress, masks and other accessories. Pick up a stick-on Sal-

NUGGETY CHRISTMAS NOSH

When Christmas comes, specialist pastry stores fill with *turrón*, the traditional holiday temptation (and tooth-rotter). Essentially nougat, it comes in all sorts of varieties, although at the base is a sticky almond concoction. Softer blocks are known as *turrón de Valencia* and a harder version as *turrón de Gijón*. You can find it year-round, but for the best wait until Christmas and check out stores like **Planelles** (☎ 93 317 34 39; Avinguda del Portal de l'Àngel 27; 10am-9pm Mon-Sat, 4-9pm Sun & holidays; M Catalunya). It also does great ice creams and *orxata*, the summer tiger-nut drink from Valencia.

vador Dalí moustache, or ride out on a monocycle in a devil's outfit.

ESCRIBÀ *Food & Drink*

☎ 93 301 60 27; www.escriba.es; La Rambla de Sant Josep 83; 🕒 9am-9pm; Ⓜ Liceu

Chocolates, dainty pastries and mouthwatering cakes can be lapped up behind the Modernista mosaic façade here. This Barcelona favourite is owned by the Escribà family, a name synonymous with sinfully good sweet things.

FC BOTIGA
Football Paraphernalia

☎ 93 269 15 32; Carrer de Jaume I 18; 🕒 10am-9pm; Ⓜ Jaume I

Need a Ronaldinho football jersey, a blue and burgundy ball, or any other soccer paraphernalia pertaining to what many locals consider the greatest team in the world? This is a convenient spot to load up without traipsing to the stadium.

GANIVETERIA ROCA
Homeware

☎ 93 302 12 41; www.ganiveteriaroca.es; Plaça del Pi 3; 🕒 9.45am-1.30pm & 4.15-8pm Mon-Fri, 10am-2pm & 5-8pm Sat; Ⓜ Liceu

If it needs to be cut, clipped, snipped, trimmed, shorn, shaved or cropped, you'll find the perfect instrument at this classic gentlemen's shop, going strong since 1911. You'll also find wine and kitchen accessories here.

GEMMA POVO *Antiques*

☎ 93 301 34 76; www.gemmapovo.com; Carrer dels Banys Nous 5-7; 🕒 9.30am-2.30pm Mon-Fri, 10am-2pm & 5-8.30pm Sat; Ⓜ Liceu

Several streets in the heart of old Barcelona bustle with decades of collected furniture, gewgaws and other oddities. Rummagers should head for Carrer de la Palla (B2) and Carrer dels Banys Nous (B3) as a start. In the latter is this interesting stop, where you'll find items in the house speciality: wrought iron.

GOTHAM *Antiques*

☎ 93 412 46 47; www.gotham-bcn.com; Carrer de Cervantes 7; 🕒 10.30am-2pm & 5-8.30pm Mon-Sat; Ⓜ Jaume I

This great retro shop specialises in furniture and furnishings from the 1950s, '60s and '70s, but you'll also find an assortment of older stuff as well as up-to-the-minute new designs – a curious all-sorts mixture.

JOGUINES FOYÈ *Toys*

☎ 93 302 03 89; Carrer dels Banys Nous 13; 🕒 10am-2pm & 4.30-8pm Mon-Fri, 10am-2pm & 5-8pm Sat; Ⓜ Liceu

The best toy shop in the old quarter stocks lots of traditional playthings, such as tin toys, creepy porcelain dolls and music boxes, as well as a range of modern gizmos.

MARKET SQUARES

Make the most of Barcelona's many markets:

> Plaça Nova (B2) Antiques and bric-a-brac on Thursday
> Plaça de Sant Josep Oriol (B3) Arts and crafts on Saturday and Sunday
> Plaça del Pi (A3) Artisanal food products Friday to Sunday every fortnight
> Plaça Reial (B4) Stamps and coins on Sunday morning
> Mercat de Sant Antoni (Map p65, A4) Old maps, stamps, books and cards on Sunday morning

LA CONDONERIA

Condoms & Erotica

☎ 93 302 77 21; www.lacondoneria.com; Plaça de Sant Josep Oriol 3; 10.30am-2pm & 4-8.30pm Mon-Sat; M Liceu

Spaniards call them *consoladores,* a much nicer word than dildos. If you've left yours at home, this is a cheerful and utterly untacky spot to find a replacement. While you're at it, stock up on orange-scented lube and perhaps a packet of lurid green ribbed condoms.

LE BOUDOIR

Lingerie & Erotica

☎ 93 302 52 81; www.leboudoir.net; Carrer de la Canuda 21; 10am-8.30pm Mon-Fri, 10.30am-9pm Sun; M Catalunya

It's not just about stylish, matt-black vibrators and penis rings. In this sensually sexy shop you'll find anything from fluffy handcuffs to night masks, incense to whips and candy bras to books on the arts of love and seduction.

L'HERBORISTERIA DEL REI

Herbs

☎ 93 318 05 12; www.herboristeriadelrei.com; Carrer del Vidre 1; 5-8pm Mon, 10am-2pm & 5-8pm Tue-Sat; M Liceu

This soothing shop is framed by a grand balcony and lined with the tiny drawers of herbal specimens that have kept it in business since 1823. The shop took the name when it became court herbalist to Queen Isabel II.

MERCAT DE LA BOQUERIA

Market

☎ 93 318 25 84; La Rambla de Sant Josep 91; 8am-8.30pm Mon-Sat; M Liceu

One of Europe's best and most famous markets (see p30), this bustling produce hall is laden with atmosphere, colour and all the ingredients that make Spanish cuisine a favourite at the kitchen table.

OBACH *Millinery*

☎ 93 318 40 94; Carrer del Call 2; 9.30am-1.30pm & 4-8pm Mon-Fri, 10am-2pm & 4.30-8pm Sat; M Liceu

If the hat ever makes a comeback, the Obach family of milliners, in the heart of what was once the Jewish quarter, stands to make a killing. Since 1924 it has been providing gentlemen with apparel for their scones.

PAPABUBBLE *Food & Drink*

☎ 93 268 86 25; www.papabubble.com; Carrer Ample 28; 🕑 10am-2pm & 4-8.30pm Tue-Fri, 10am-8.30pm Sat, 11am-7.30pm Sun, closed Aug; Ⓜ Drassanes

They really make the boiled sweets here in front of your eyes! Sample the wares and try to resist walking away without a big jar of humbugs and other multicoloured wonders, or a house speciality, life-size candy phalluses.

SESTIENDA *Gay Erotica*

☎ 93 318 86 76; www.sestienda.com; Carrer d'En Rauric 11; 🕑 10am-8.30pm Mon-Sat; Ⓜ Liceu

At this exclusively gay sex shop you can get your gay map of the city along with all the apparatus required for a happy holiday. It's been in business since 1981 and was the first of its kind in Spain.

BOUTIQUES GALORE ALONG CARRER D'AVINYÓ

Not so many years back, this was a lugubrious lane. What a transformation! Commencing at Carrer Ample (D4) and working your way to Carrer de Ferran (B3), it is festooned with small fashion boutiques, such as Zsu Zsa (No 50), Urbana (No 39), Loft Avignon (No 22) and many others. The startling, narrow, gaudy neoclassical Llotja, about halfway along, is a design and art school.

EAT

AGUT *Catalan* €€

☎ 93 315 17 09; Carrer d'En Gignàs 16; 🕑 lunch & dinner Tue-Sat, lunch Sun; Ⓜ Jaume I; ⊠

This friendly family-run restaurant appeals to a sedate crowd that digs its traditional and robust Catalan fare. The *suquet de rap* (monkfish stew) is finger-licking good, but there are succulent sirloin steaks for greater sustenance.

BAR CELTA *Tapas* €

☎ 93 315 00 06; Carrer de la Mercè 16; 🕑 noon-midnight; Ⓜ Drassanes

The stormy Atlantic in Spain's northwest yields seafood goodies that wind up in bars like this as tapas. *Pulpo a la gallega* – boiled octopus in a slightly spicy oil mix – is one. Accompany with a shallow ceramic cup of crisp Ribeiro white.

CAFÈ DE L'ACADÈMIA *Catalan* €€€

☎ 93 319 82 53; Carrer de Lledó 1; 🕑 lunch & dinner Mon-Fri; Ⓜ Jaume I; ⊠

An old favourite with hungry, hard-working public servants in the nearby Ajuntament, this café never fails to satisfy their demands. The key to its success is a solid grounding in well-prepared local cuisine with the occasional inventive twist. The atmosphere hums good-naturedly at lunchtime but is rather more subdued and romantic in the evening.

CAFÈ DE L'ÒPERA *Café* €

☎ 93 302 41 80; La Rambla 74; 9am-3am; M Liceu;

This busy café is the most atmospheric on La Rambla, having stood the test of time. Bohemians and their buddies mingle with tourists beneath Art Deco images of opera heroines etched into mirrors.

CAFÈ ZURICH *Café* €

☎ 93 317 91 53; Carrer de Pelai 39; 8am-midnight; M Catalunya;

The original 1920s Cafè Zurich was one of the city's landmark meeting places, but it was torn down in 1997 to make way for the department store now on this corner. The café's pseudoclassic replacement may not have the same charm, but the tables are perfectly placed for watching the world go by.

CAN CULLERETES *Catalan* €€

☎ 93 317 30 22; Carrer d'En Quintana 5; lunch & dinner Tue-Sat, lunch Sun; M Liceu;

Founded in 1786, Barcelona's oldest restaurant is still going strong, with tourists and locals flocking to enjoy its rambling interior, old-fashioned tiled décor, and enormous helpings of traditional Catalan food. Service with a snarl is compensated for by the timeless setting.

COMETACINC *Fusion* €€

☎ 93 310 15 58; Carrer del Cometa 5; dinner Wed-Mon; M Jaume I;

This atmospheric medieval den turns out an ever-changing menu of items that transgress all culinary boundaries. Salads come in unexpected mixes, or you could opt for a pseudo-Thai dish. The candle-lit tables over two floors add a touch of romantic intimacy.

EL PARAGUAYO *South American* €€

☎ 93 302 14 41; Carrer del Parc 1; lunch & dinner Tue-Sun; M Drassanes

Forget about Catalan refinements, teasing tapas or avant-garde pretensions. Here the word is meat – great juicy slabs of the stuff. Tuck into all sorts of tasty cuts of beef, pork and other flesh in this little Latin American oasis.

LOS CARACOLES *Catalan* €€

☎ 93 302 31 85; Carrer dels Escudellers 14; lunch & dinner; M Drassanes;

This 19th-century tavern is the Barri Gòtic's most picturesque restaurant. It's famous for spit-roasted chickens and, as the

Ramon & Aurora Bofarull,
Co-owners, Los Caracoles restaurant

You've been in business for a while. Ramon e're the fifth generation. 't's been going since 1 . **And the snails *(caracoles)* are the best?** Ramon They're good. e've been working with a supplier in Vic for generations. Aurora The restaurant was called Casa Bofarull but, in our grandfather's time, theatre-goers to the Liceu would say let's go for snails So the name changed. **Some folks in Barcelona say the restaurant is too touristy.** Ramon In the evening we get many foreigners, but lunch is mostly local regulars. **You used to attract many famous guests, right?** Ramon Giorgio Armani was here last night **Where do you eat out?** Aurora e both like apanese. And I love Cal Pep (p). **Would you live anywhere else?** Aurora Live Nooo. Ramon I don't think so. If I had to start from scratch, I wouldn't mind Sydney.

MENÚ DEL DÍA

Most restaurants offer a set lunch menu (*menú del día,* or meal of the day), which usually consists of three courses and a drink. The meals typically cost half or less than ordering à la carte.

name suggests, snails (from the town of Vic, north of Barcelona). Largely frequented by tourists in the evenings, it is still a highly atmospheric spot (and the snails are not bad at all!).

PLA *Fusion* €€€

93 412 65 52; Carrer de Bellafila 5; dinner; M Jaume I;

The most chic choice in the Gothic quarter, Pla has black-and-white menus featuring photos of staff in action, mainly serving superb and innovative modern Mediterranean dishes with an Asian twist.

RESTAURANT PITARRA *Catalan* €€€

93 301 16 47; Carrer d'Avinyó 56; lunch & dinner Mon-Sat, closed Aug; M Drassanes;

Time stood still in this restaurant, which was established in 1890 and occupies the house where the 19th-century playwright Serafi Pitarra penned most of his work. The walls are crammed with old art, clocks and photos of local politicians who have been regaled with things such as pig trotters' meat.

SHUNKA *Japanese* €€€

93 412 49 91; Carrer dels Sagristans 5; lunch & dinner Tue-Sun; M Jaume I

Shunka is a cut above Barcelona's Oriental average. The presence of Japanese punters is reassuring, and the open-plan kitchen also inspires confidence – you can keep an eye on what they're doing with your tempura and sashimi.

DRINK

BARCELONA PIPA CLUB *Bar*

93 302 47 32; Plaça Reial 3; 11pm-4am; M Liceu

Ring the buzzer at one of the most intriguing bars in the city. It's a genuine pipe-smokers' club by day and transforms into a dim, laid-back and incurably cool bar at night. Closing times are a matter of whim.

CAFÉ ROYALE *Bar*

93 412 14 33; Carrer Nou de Zurbano 3; 6pm-2.30am; M Liceu

These are some of the most sought-after sofas in Barcelona, perfect for chilling out with warm lighting, a good-looking crowd, and irresistible soul, funk and bossa fusions. It gets terribly packed with visitors at the weekend. That's no surprise, as it's one of the hippest early-evening dance options in town.

CLUB ROSA *Bar*

Carrer d'En Rauric 23; 8pm-2.30am Sun-Thu, to 3am Fri & Sat; M Liceu

A Gothic bar for the Gothic quarter – well, with a couple of baroque touches (such as the heavy gilt-framed mirror). An Addams family collection of dark paintings, low-lit lamps, dripping candles, chilled music and even cooler cocktails create a deliciously conspiratorial atmosphere.

MANCHESTER *Bar*

627 733081; www.manchesterbar.com; Carrer de Milans 5; 7pm-2.30am Sun-Thu, to 3am Fri & Sat; M Liceu

Feeling nostalgic for the sounds of Manchester? This is the place to fill up on Depeche Mode, The Smiths, Radiohead and other bands associated with the city. Inside, red is the predominant shade and cocktails the principal tipple. It has a sister joint in the El Raval neighbourhood.

MILK BAR & BISTRO *Bar*

93 268 09 22; Carrer d'En Gignàs 21; 6.30pm-3am daily & noon-4pm brunch Sun; M Jaume I

Smiling bar staff, 1920s wallpaper, comfortable lounges and gently wafting chill-out music all conspire to create an inviting ambience for a languorous tipple or three. The cocktails at this establishment are inventive, light meals are available and the Sunday brunch is a formidable hangover cure.

SCHILLING *Bar*

93 317 67 87; Carrer de Ferran 23; [illegible].30am-2.30am Mon-Sat, noon-2.30am Sun; M Liceu

No it's not new, nor is it hidden away anywhere, and increasingly it is filled with out-of-towners rather than locals. But this gay-friendly favourite remains a great place to sip on a glass of wine or two before heading out into a more adventurous night. Grab a tiny round marble table if you can and ignore the somewhat frosty service.

SOUL CLUB *Club*

93 302 70 26; Carrer Nou de Sant Francesc 7; 10pm-2.30am Mon-Thu, to 3am Fri & Sat; M Drassanes

This backstreet treasure (still known to many as Dot Light Club) has a cosy bar at the front for an intimate chat (on the single sofa), and an equally diminutive, congenial dance floor out the back.

SUGAR *Bar*

www.sugarbarcelona.com; Carrer d'En Rauric 21; 8pm-2.30am Sun-Thu, to 3am Fri-Sat; M Liceu

This funky little cave is proof that you can go a long way with very little. Throw a few cushions (it could do with more) around the entrance cubby hole and benches, add a bar, DJ, red lighting, cocktails and stir. A fun place to hang out before clubbing.

PLAY

CLUB FELLINI *Club*

687 969825; www.clubfellini.com; La Rambla 27; admission €15 midnight-5am Mon-Sat May-Sep, Mon & Thu-Sat Oct-Apr; M Drassanes

Nestled in between peep shows and a striptease hall, this longtime club has undergone an overhaul and name change. Three separate spaces (the Bad

Flamenco dancer, Sala Tarantos

Room, the Red Room and the Mirror Hall) blare out anything from house to '80s disco. On slow Mondays, come along for rock 'n' roll and indie rock at the Nasty Mondays session.

GRAN TEATRE DEL LICEU *Opera*

93 485 99 00; www.liceubarcelona.com; La Rambla dels Caputxins 51-59; admission €7.50-150; box office 2-8.30pm Mon-Fri, 1hr before show Sat & Sun; M Liceu;

Some good can come of disasters. Fire in 1994 destroyed this old dame of opera but the reconstruction has left Barcelona with one of the most technologically advanced theatres in the world. It remains a fabulously plush setting for your favourite aria.

HARLEM JAZZ CLUB *Live Music*

93 310 07 55; Carrer de la Comtessa de Sobradiel 8; admission up to €10; 8pm-4am Tue-Thu & Sun, to 5am Fri & Sat; M Jaume I

Deep in the Barri Gòtic, this smoky dive is the first stop for jazz aficionados. Sessions include traditional and contemporary jazz along with creative fusions from around the world. They usually put on more than one cosy session an evening.

JAMBOREE *Live Music*

93 319 17 89; www.masimas.com/jamboree; Plaça Reial 17; admission up to €10; 10.30pm-5am; M Liceu

This cavernous place with multiple low-ceiling spaces has been bringing headline jazz and blues acts to Barcelona for decades. Gigs tend to start at 11pm and end by 2am, at which time it converts into a club cranking out mostly funk and hip-hop.

NEW YORK *Club*

93 318 87 30; Carrer dels Escudellers 5; admission €10; midnight-5am Thu-Sun; M Drassanes

Until the mid-1990s, this street was lined with dingy bars of ill-repute. New York was one of them but has been reborn as a popular old-town club space. Friday night is best, with anything from reggae to rock steady.

SALA TARANTOS *Flamenco*

93 318 30 67; http://masimas.com/tarantos; Plaça Reial 17; admission from €5; 10pm-5am Mon-Sat; M Liceu

Locals and tourists get hot and steamy with flamenco, Latin and salsa sessions here. There's a middling flamenco *tablao* (show), usually between 8.30pm and 11pm. Later on it converts into a club with Latin sounds. You can wander over to Jamboree (with which it is connected) next door.

>EL RAVAL

El Raval (and especially its lower red-light half, known as the Barri Xinès, or Chinese Quarter) was long an old city slum and all-round louche quarter. To some extent it still is. It is doubtless the most colourful of the three Ciutat Vella (Old Town) districts, home to a growing migrant community (above all Pakistanis and North Africans) and still a haunt for down-and-outs, prostitutes and the occasional drug dealer. At the same time, the opening of the Macba contemporary art gallery, CCCB cultural centre and now the enormous philosophy and history faculties of the Universitat de Barcelona have injected new life. A housing programme and luxury hotel complex are also in the pipeline.

The massive arrival of local students and tourists is also transforming the district. Classic bars and restaurants have been joined by all manner of sparkling new places, some snooty, some grungy. Awaiting discovery are a Romanesque church, maritime museum and one of Gaudí's early commissions.

EL RAVAL

SEE

Name	No	Grid
Antic Hospital de la Santa Creu	1	C4
Centre de Cultura Contemporània de Barcelona	2	B3
Església de Sant Pau del Camp	3	B5
Museu d'Art Contemporani de Barcelona	4	B3
Palau Güell	5	D4

SHOP

Name	No	Grid
Castelló	6	C2
Etnomusic	7	C3
La Portorriqueña	8	B3

EAT

Name	No	Grid
Bar Central	9	C4
Bar Kasparo	10	B3
Biblioteca	11	C4
Biocenter	12	B3
Ca L'Isidre	13	B5
Casa Leopoldo	14	B4
Elisabets	15	B3
Granja Viader	16	C3
Sesamo	17	A4

DRINK

Name	No	Grid
23 Robadors	18	C4
Bar Marsella	19	C5
Bar Muy Buenas	20	B4
Bar Pastís	21	D5
Casa Almirall	22	B3
Kentucky	23	D5
London Bar	24	C5
Zentraus	25	C5

PLAY

Name	No	Grid
La Paloma	26	A3
Moog	27	D5

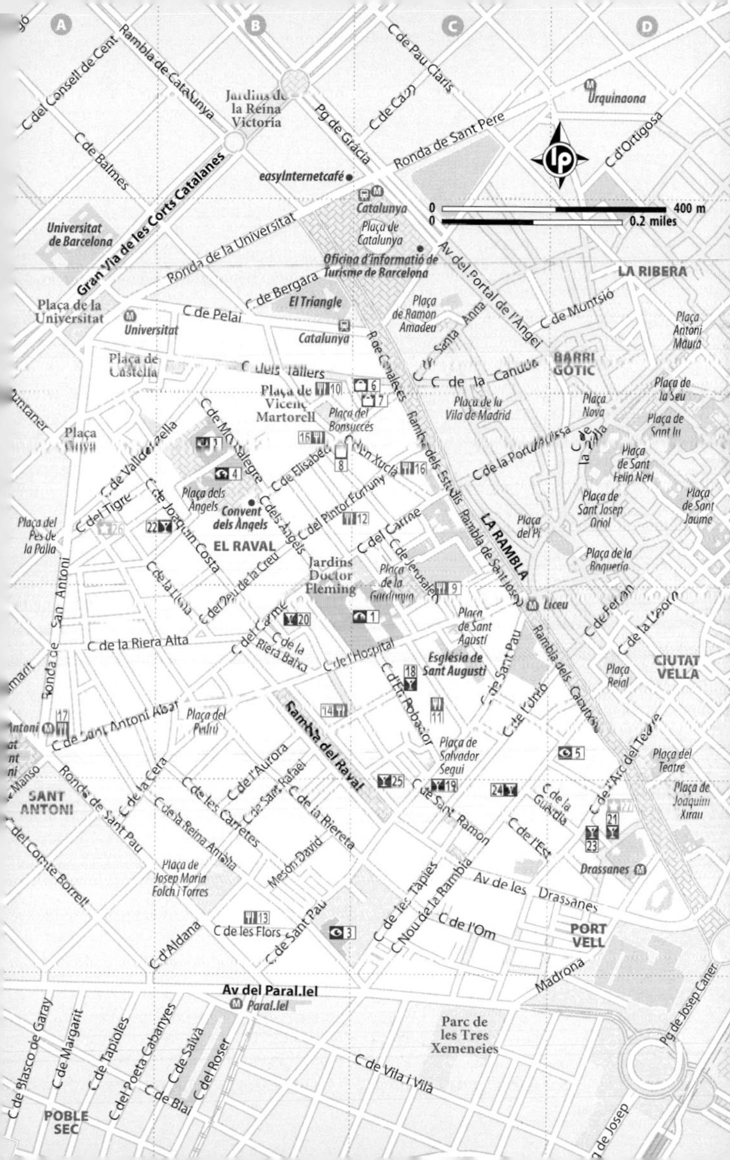

A
B
C
D
Jardins de la Reina Victoria
Urquinaona
Universitat de Barcelona
easyInternetcafé
Catalunya
Plaça de Catalunya
0 400 m
0 0.2 miles
Oficina d'informació de Turisme de Barcelona
LA RIBERA
Plaça de la Universitat
Universitat
El Triangle
Plaça de Ramon Amadeu
Catalunya
Plaça Antoni Maura
Plaça de Castella
BARRI GÒTIC
Plaça de Vicenç Martorell
Plaça del Bonsuccés
Plaça de la Vila de Madrid
Plaça Nova
Plaça de la Seu
Plaça de Sant Iu
Plaça de Sant Felip Neri
Plaça dels Àngels
Convent dels Àngels
Plaça del Pes de la Palla
EL RAVAL
LA RAMBLA
Plaça del Pi
Plaça de Sant Josep Oriol
Plaça de Sant Jaume
Jardins Doctor Fleming
Plaça de la Gardunya
Plaça de la Boqueria
Liceu
Plaça de Sant Agustí
Església de Sant Agustí
CIUTAT VELLA
Plaça Reial
Plaça del Pedró
Plaça de Salvador Seguí
Plaça del Teatre
Plaça de Joaquim Xirau
SANT ANTONI
Plaça de Josep Maria Folch i Torres
Drassanes
PORT VELL
Av del Paral.lel
Paral.lel
Parc de les Tres Xemeneies
POBLE SEC
Rambla de Catalunya
C del Consell de Cent
C de Pau Claris
C de Casp
Pg de Gràcia
Ronda de Sant Pere
C d'Ortigosa
C de Balmes
Gran Via de les Corts Catalanes
Ronda de la Universitat
Av del Portal de l'Àngel
C de Bergara
C de Pelai
C de Montsió
C dels Tallers
C de la Canuda
C de Santa Anna
Rambla dels Estudis
C de Montalegre
C d'En Xuclà
C de la Portaferrissa
C de Valldonzella
C del Tigre
C de Joaquín Costa
C dels Àngels
C del Pintor Fortuny
C del Carme
C de Jerusalem
Rambla de Sant Josep
C de la Riera Alta
C de la Riera Baixa
C de l'Hospital
C de Sant Pau
C de Ferran
C de la Unió
Rambla dels Caputxins
Ronda de Sant Antoni
C de Sant Antoni Abat
Rambla del Raval
C d'En Robador
C de Sant Ramon
C de l'Arc del Teatre
Ronda de Sant Pau
C de la Cera
C de l'Aurora
C de Sant Rafael
C de la Riereta
C de les Carretes
C de la Reina Amàlia
C de la Guàrdia
C de l'Est
C del Comte Borrell
Mesón David
C de les Tàpies
C Nou de la Rambla
Av de les Drassanes
C de les Flors
C de l'Om
C d'Aldana
Madrona
Pg de Josep Carner
C de Blasco de Garay
C de Margarit
C de Tapioles
C del Poeta Cabanyes
C de Salvà
C del Roser
C de Blai
C de Vila i Vilà

SEE

ANTIC HOSPITAL DE LA SANTA CREU

☎ 93 270 23 00; Carrer de l'Hospital 56; library 9am-8pm Mon-Fri, to 2pm Sat; M Liceu

Gaudí died at this 15th-century hospital, which now houses Catalonia's national library (take a look at the magnificent vaulted reading room) and an arts school. It has a delightful, if somewhat dilapidated, colonnaded courtyard with a chirpy café. The **chapel** (☎ 93 442 71 71; www.bcn.es/virreinaexposicions; noon-2pm & 4-8pm Tue-Sat, 11am-2pm Sun & holidays) is used for temporary exhibitions.

CENTRE DE CULTURA CONTEMPORÀNIA DE BARCELONA (CCCB)

☎ 93 306 41 00; www.cccb.org; Carrer de Montalegre 5; adult/student €6/4.40; 11am-8pm Tue-Sat, to 3pm Sun & holidays 21 Jun-21 Sep, 11am-2pm & 4-8pm Tue, Thu & Fri, 11am-8pm Wed & Sat, 11am-7pm Sun & holidays 22 Sep-20 Jun; M Universitat; ♿

Loved by locals, this dynamic, multi-use cultural centre occupies the shell of an 18th-century hospice, with sgraffiti décor in the main courtyard, and hosts a constantly changing programme of exhibitions on urban design, 20th-century arts, architecture and the city itself.

FAT CAT

Gat, the tubby tabby in the Rambla del Raval, is the work of Colombian artist Fernando Botero and was unveiled in 1992. The statue's biggest headache are the vandals who occasionally break off his whiskers!

ESGLÉSIA DE SANT PAU DEL CAMP

☎ 93 441 00 01; Carrer de Sant Pau 101; cloister 10am-2pm; M Paral.lel

Barcelona's oldest church, St Paul in the Fields was founded by monks in the 9th century. Although the squat, rural-looking building shows its age, it has some wonderful Visigothic sculptural decoration on its doorway and a fine Romanesque cloister.

MUSEU D'ART CONTEMPORANI DE BARCELONA (MACBA)

☎ 93 412 08 10; www.macba.es; Plaça dels Àngels 1; admission full ticket/permanent collection only/temporary exhibition only €7.20/6/4; 11am-7.30pm Mon, Wed-Fri, 10am-8pm Sat, 10am-3pm Sun & holidays; M Universitat; ♿

The ever-expanding contemporary art collection of the Macba starts in the Gothic chapel of the Convent dels Àngels and continues in the main gleaming-white building across the square. It shines as a stage for the best of Catalan, Spanish and international contemporary art. What's on show is in constant, restless flux, although in the chapel you are more likely to see established names such as Alexander Calder and Antoni Tàpies.

PALAU GÜELL

☎ 93 317 39 74; Carrer Nou de la Rambla 3-5; closed for renovation until 2007; M Liceu

With this commission for wealthy patron Eusebi Güell, Antoni Gaudí first showed what he was capable of. Sombre compared with his later whims, it is still a characteristic riot of styles (Gothic, Islamic, Art Nouveau) and materials. Following the civil war, the police tortured political prisoners in the basement. Up

Gaudí's chimney pots, Palau Güell

two floors you reach the main hall and its annexes. The hall is a parabolic pyramid – each wall an arch stretching up three floors and coming together to form a dome. The roof is a Gaudian riot of ceramic colour and fanciful design in the chimney pots.

SHOP

CASTELLÓ *Music*

☎ 93 302 59 46; www.discoscastello.es; Carrer dels Tallers 7; 10am-8.30pm Mon-Sat; M Catalunya

This family-run chain has been tickling the ear lobes of Catalans since 1935, and has five stores in El Raval. Each specialises in a different genre so, between them, you're bound to hit the right chord. Aside from the main branch, try Carrer dels Tallers 3 for classical music, No 9 for alternative, hip-hop and other contemporary sounds and No 79, another general store.

ETNOMUSIC *Music*

☎ 93 301 18 84; www.etnomusic.com; Carrer del Bonsuccés 6; 5-8pm Mon, 11am-2pm & 5-8pm Tue-Sat; M Catalunya

From flamenco to samba and a whole lot in between, this is your best bet for music from around the globe.

PRE-LOVED ON CARRER DE LA RIERA BAIXA

Looking for fashion bargains, perfect for passing unnoticed in this 'hood? In little more than 100m, starting on Carrer de l'Hospital (B4) and finishing on Carrer del Carme (B4), you'll find the best part of a dozen clothes shops, mostly secondhand. For some variety, a couple of secondhand record stores and the nicely restored and now Argentine-run Bar Resolis are thrown in to the bargain.

LA PORTORRIQUEÑA *Food & Drink*

☎ 93 317 34 38; Carrer d'En Xuclà 25; 9am-2pm & 5-8pm Mon-Fri, 9am-2pm Sat; M Catalunya

Forget Starbucks, this is coffee. Beans from around the world are freshly ground before your eyes in the combination of your choice. This place has been in the coffee business here since 1902. It also purveys all sorts of chocolate goodies.

EAT

BAR CENTRAL *Catalan* €€

☎ 93 301 10 98; Mercat de la Boqueria; lunch Mon-Sat; M Liceu

This no-nonsense eatery towards the back of Barcelona's emblematic produce market is one of the best of several for a hearty lunch.

Marketeers, local workers and the occasional curious tourist jostle for a stool. Go for the grilled fish of the day or perhaps some chunky *mandonguilles* (meatballs).

BAR KASPARO

Mediterranean €€

☎ 93 302 20 72; Plaça de Vicenç Martorell 4; 9am-10pm; M Catalunya
Pull up a stainless-steel pew for terrace dining beneath vaults at this friendly Australian-run place, on the corner of a pleasant square with swings for the kids. It does a sturdy line in snacks, mixed salads, filled rolls and hot dishes that change daily.

BIBLIOTECA

Mediterranean €€€

☎ 93 412 62 21; Carrer de la Junta del Comerç 28; lunch & dinner Tue-Sat; M Liceu
In a long ground-floor setting, with bare brick walls and a stylishly simple white décor, the 'Library' presents a changing menu of mixed dishes. The food is rooted in a mix of Navarran and general Mediterranean cooking. The *menú del día* (€9) is worth a detour.

BIOCENTER *Vegetarian €*

☎ 93 301 45 83; www.biocenter.es; Carrer del Pintor Fortuny 25; lunch only Mon-Tue, lunch & dinner Wed-Fri, dinner only Sat; M Liceu; ⊠ V
You share your table with whomever at this large and friendly veggie restaurant, serving a great assortment of salads, casseroles and seasonal vegetables cooked using various techniques from around the world. A *combinat* is a good option – you select one of the hot meals of the day and then heap on salad from the buffet out the back.

CA L'ISIDRE *Catalan* €€€

☎ 93 441 11 39; Carrer de les Flors 12; lunch & dinner Mon-Sat; M Paral.lel
Every morning, chefs from this seemingly unremarkable, back-street restaurant wander across to the bounteous Mercat de la Boqueria to stock up on the raw materials for the day's cooking. Grand, traditionally decorated dining areas sweep back from the entrance, ready to accommodate you for some fine fresh-fish dishes.

CASA LEOPOLDO

Catalan €€€€

☎ 93 441 30 14; Carrer de Sant Rafael 24; lunch & dinner Tue-Sat, lunch Sun; M Liceu; ⊠
Several rambling dining areas, all of them sporting magnificent tiled walls and exposed timber-beam ceilings, make this a fine option for lovers of local tradition. The seafood menu is extensive

and the wine list is strong on the local product.

ELISABETS *Catalan* €€

93 317 58 26; Carrer de Elisabets 2-4; lunch & dinner Mon-Sat; M Catalunya;

Thank God places like this haven't been swept away by the rising tide of gleaming, trendy, could-be-anywhere-in-Soho avant-garde locales. What about good old food that hits the comfort spot? The walls are lined with old radio sets, and the lunch menu varies daily. Try the throaty venison flavour of the *ragú de jabalí* (wild-boar stew).

GRANJA VIADER *Dairy Bar* €

93 318 34 86; Carrer d'En Xuclà 4; 9am-1.45pm & 5-8.45pm Tue-Sat, 5-8.45pm Mon; M Liceu;

The fifth generation of the same family runs this atmospheric milk bar and café, set up in 1873 as the first to bring farm freshness to the city. They invented *cacaolat,* the chocolate-and-skimmed-milk drink now popular all over Spain, and continue to be innovative purveyors of all things milky.

SESAMO *Vegetarian* €

93 441 64 11; www.sesamo-bcn.com; Carrer de Sant Antoni Abat 52; lunch & dinner Mon & Tue & Thu-Sat, lunch Sun; M Sant Antoni; V

For 'food without beasts', this relaxed corner eatery attracts all sorts. Drop by for juices and pastries at breakfast, a three-course set lunch (€7) or dinner. Wafting electronica is almost soothing and nice touches include the home-baked bread and cakes.

DRINK

23 ROBADORS *Bar*

Carrer d'En Robador 23; 8pm-2.30am Tue-Sun; M Liceu

You may find the door ajar on this still slightly dodgy street (but a big clean up is under way). Push it open and step inside a funky little bar with exposed-brick walls and timber beams, where dressing down is the rule. Out the back you'll hear some light jazz on Wednesdays and flamenco on Sundays (9pm to midnight).

BAR MARSELLA *Bar*

Carrer de Sant Pau 65; 9pm-2am Mon-Thu, to 3am Fri & Sat; M Liceu

This place looks like it hasn't had a lick of paint since it opened in 1820. Assorted chandeliers, tiles and mirrors decorate its one rambunctious room, which on weekends is packed to its rickety rafters with a cheerful mishmash of shady characters, slumming uptowners and Erasmus students, who all stop by to try the absinthe.

BAR MUY BUENAS *Bar*

☎ 93 442 50 53; Carrer del Carme 63; 🕙 7.30am-2.30am; M Liceu

What started life as a late-19th-century milk bar is now lacking the milk. The Modernista décor and relaxed company make this a great spot for a quiet *mojito* (rum and lime cocktail), perhaps some live music and Middle Eastern nibbles.

BAR PASTÍS *Bar*

☎ 93 318 79 80; Carrer de Santa Mònica 4; 🕙 7.30pm-3am Tue-Sun; M Drassanes

Although French cabaret *chanson* dominates, you might just as easily find yourself confronted by a little bossa nova or tango, depending on when you wander into this cluttered bar, in business since WWII.

Bar Marsella

CASA ALMIRALL *Bar*

☎ 93 318 99 17; Carrer de Joaquín Costa 33; 7pm-2.30am; M Universitat

People have been boozing here since 1860, which makes it the oldest continuously functioning bar in Barcelona. Delightfully dishevelled, it still has its original Modernista bar.

KENTUCKY *Bar*

☎ 93 318 28 78; Carrer de l'Arc del Teatre 11; 10pm-3am Tue-Sat; M Drassanes

Once a popular hang-out for US navy personnel when the boys were in town, this narrow exercise in Americana kitsch is a smoke-filled, surreal drinking dive, almost always packed to the rafters.

DJ 'Ramon', La Paloma

RUNNING THE GAUNTLET ON CARRER DE SANT RAMON

A trip to the legendary Bar Marsella (p70) can also involve a brief walk on the wild side. Along its flank runs Carrer de Sant Ramon, though there's nothing very saintly about this street. In two short blocks you'll see an international brigade of streetwalkers, their pimps, drug dealers and occasionally just a bunch of older locals animatedly discussing football in the middle of the road.

LONDON BAR *Bar*

☎ 93 318 52 61; Carrer Nou de la Rambla 34; 7.30pm-3am; M Drassanes

In the heart of the once-notorious Barri Xinès district, this bar was founded in 1910 as a hangout for circus hands, and drew the likes of Picasso and Miró in search of local colour. With the occasional band playing out the back and a wonderful mix of local customers and travellers, it remains a classic.

ZENTRAUS *Bar*

☎ 93 443 80 78; www.zentraus.com; Rambla del Raval 41; noon-2.30am; M Liceu

Get down into this cheerfully bump-and-grind, semisubterranean dance club. Drum 'n' bass earlier in the week rises to a deep house crescendo on Saturdays, and drops back into a mellow mix on Sundays. It puts on food, too. Only problem is the place closes just when you're getting into the swing.

PLAY

LA PALOMA *Club*

☎ 93 301 68 97; www.lapaloma-bcn.com; Carrer del Tigre 27; admission €6-10; midnight-5am Thu & Fri, 2am-5am Sat; M Universitat

The 100-year-old La Paloma is a unique local institution and an essential night out. The evening starts early with the band playing cha-chas and tangos to a chirpy crowd of middle-aged and retired couples. From midnight it sheds its nostalgia skin to become one of the hippest dance dives around town.

MOOG *Club*

☎ 93 301 72 82; www.masimas.com/moog; Carrer de l'Arc del Teatre 3; admission €8; 11.30pm-5am; M Drassanes

Moog (named after the synthesiser) is reliable for techno and electronica, and always packed with a young, enthusiastic crowd. Bigger in stature than in size, it attracts lots of big-name DJs. Upstairs specialises in indie retro pop numbers and is better for conversationalists.

>LA RIBERA

An integral part of the Barri Gòtic until it was split off by Via Laietana in the early 1900s, La Ribera was Barcelona's economic powerhouse. Rich merchants lived on Carrer de Montcada, home today to the Museu Picasso.

The activity was especially great around El Born, a short leafy boulevard behind Barcelona's mightiest Gothic church, Santa Maria del Mar. Until the early 1990s, a handful of sad old bars dotted the area. Today, the timeless lanes are crammed with restaurants, bars and boutiques. To the northeast stretches the green lung of Parc de la Ciutadella.

LA RIBERA

SEE

Arc de Triomf	1	D1
Església de Santa Maria del Mar	2	E5
Mercat de Santa Caterina	3	C3
Mercat del Born	4	E4
Museu Barbier-Mueller d'Art Precolombí	5	D4
Museu de la Xocolata	6	E3
Museu de Zoologia (Castell dels Tres Dragons)	7	E2
Museu Picasso	8	D4
Museu Tèxtil i d'Indumentària	9	D4
Palau de la Música Catalana	10	B3
Parc de la Ciutadella	11	G2
Zoo de Barcelona	12	G3

SHOP

Arlequí Màscares	13	D4
Casa Gispert	14	E5
Custo Barcelona	15	E5
El Magnifico	16	D5
La Botifarreria	17	E5
La Galería de Santa María Novella	18	E5
Taller Antic	19	D4
Tot Formatge	20	E4
Vila Viniteca	21	D5

EAT

Àbac	22	F5
Bubó	23	E5
Cal Pep	24	E5
Centre Cultural Euskal Etxea	25	E4
Comerç 24	26	D2
El Xampanyet	27	E4
Hofmann	28	D5
La Flauta Mágica	29	D5
Pla de la Garsa	30	D4
Santa Maria	31	E3
Set (7) Portes	32	E5

DRINK

Dr Astin	33	D5
Flow	34	E3
Gimlet	35	E4
La Fianna	36	D4
La Vinya del Senyor	37	E5
Palau de Dalmases–Espai Barroc	38	D4

PLAY

Palau de la Música Catalana ....(see 10)

Please see over for map

SEE

ARC DE TRIOMF

Passeig de Lluís Companys; M Arc de Triomf

This curious triumphal gate, with its Islamic-style brickwork, was the ceremonial entrance to the 1888 Universal Exhibition. What triumph it commemorates isn't clear – probably just getting the thing built more or less in time.

ESGLÉSIA DE SANTA MARIA DEL MAR

☎ 93 319 05 16; Plaça de Santa Maria del Mar; 9am-1.30pm & 4.30-8pm; M Jaume I

Barcelona's most powerful and beguiling Gothic temple (see also p16) stands serenely amid the swirling crowds that daily invade the El Born area, once the heart of local commerce and now devoted to local diversion.

MERCAT DE SANTA CATERINA

☎ 93 319 57 40; www.mercatsantacaterina.net; Avinguda de Francesc Cambó 16; 8am-2pm Mon, to 3.30pm Tue, Wed & Sat, to 8.30pm Thu & Fri; M Jaume I; ♿

The undulating, polychrome-tiled roof of this 21st-century produce market is a great place to shop for bananas and stop for lunch. Local architect Enric Miralles designed it on the site of its 19th-century predecessor, which itself replaced a medieval Dominican monastery.

MERCAT DEL BORN

☎ 93 319 02 22; Plaça Comercial; admission free, guided visits €3; 10am-8pm Sat, to 3pm Sun; M Barceloneta; ♿

The long-silent 19th-century Mercat del Born is destined to become a museum-cum-cultural centre after the discovery in 2000 of a whole swath of late-medieval Barcelona that had been flattened to make way for the sinister Ciutadella fortress (see Parc de la Ciutadella, p80) in the 18th century.

MUSEU BARBIER-MUELLER D'ART PRECOLOMBÍ

☎ 93 310 45 16; www.barbier-mueller.ch; Carrer de Montcada 12-14; adult/child under 16yr/student €3/free/1.50, free 1st Sun of month; 11am-7pm Tue-Fri, 10am-7pm Sat, 10am-3pm Sun & holidays; M Jaume I; ♿

In this branch of the prestigious Geneva-based Barbier-Mueller museum you'll find a sparkling assortment of art from the pre-Columbian civilisations of Central and South America. Gold glitters in the form of at times highly intricate ornamental objects, expressive masks and women's jewellery. These pieces are complemented

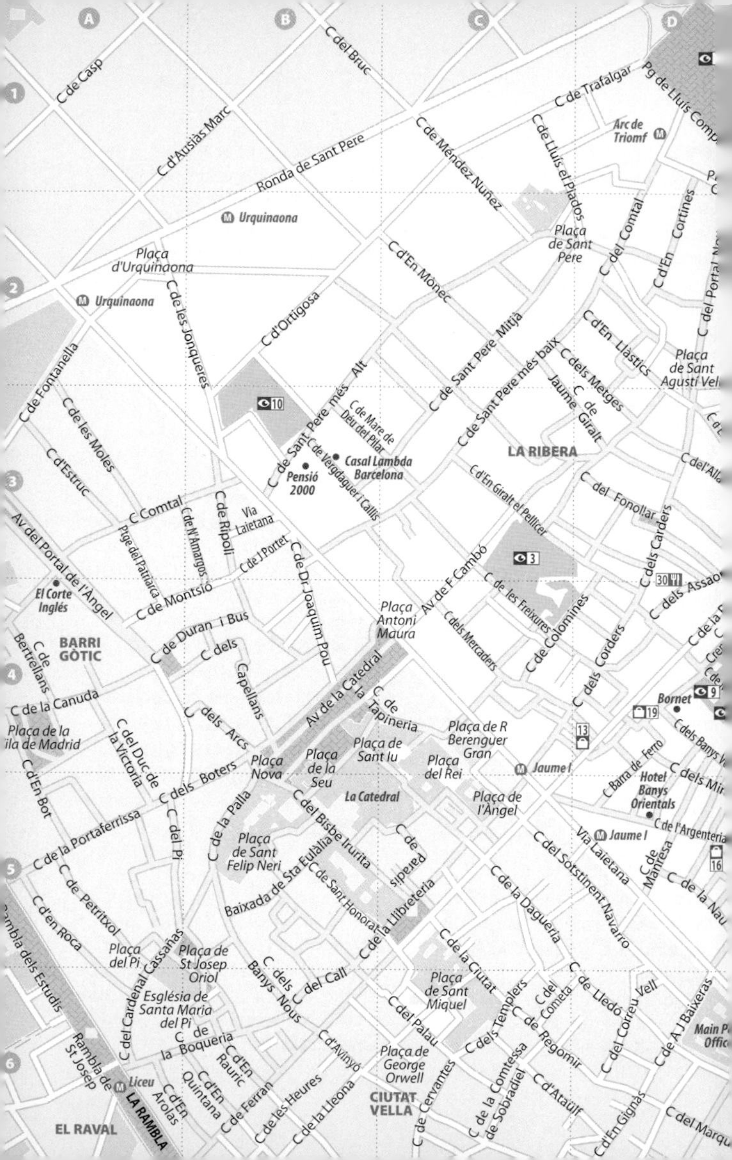

C de Casp
C d'Ausiàs Marc
C del Bruc
C de Trafalgar
Pg de Lluís Comp
Arc de Triomf
C de Lluís el Pla dos
Ronda de Sant Pere
C de Méndez Nuñez
Urquinaona
Plaça d'Urquinaona
Urquinaona
C de les Jonqueres
C d'En Mònec
Plaça de Sant Pere
C del Comtal
C d'En Cortines
C del Portal Nou
C d'Ortigosa
C de Sant Pere Mitjà
C d'En Llàstics
Plaça de Sant Agustí Vell
C de Fontanella
C de les Moles
C d'Estruc
C de Sant Pere més Alt
C de Mare de Déu del Pilar
C de Sant Pere més baix
C dels Metges
C de Jaume Giralt
LA RIBERA
C de Verdaguer i Callís
Casal Lambda Barcelona
Pensió 2000
C de l'Allada
C Comtal
Ptge del Patriarca
C de N'Amargós
C de Ripoll
Via Laietana
C de J Portet
C d'En Giralt el Pellicer
C del Fonollar
C dels Carders
Av del Portal de l'Àngel
C de Montsió
C de Dr Joaquim Pou
Av de F Cambó
C de les Freixures
C dels Assaonadors
El Corte Inglés
Plaça Antoni Maura
C dels Mercaders
C de Colomines
BARRI GÒTIC
C de Bertrellans
C de Duran i Bus
C dels Capellans
C dels Corders
Av de la Catedral
C de la Tapineria
C de la Canuda
C dels Arcs
Bornet
Plaça de la Vila de Madrid
C del Duc de la Victòria
Plaça de R Berenguer Gran
C dels Banys Vells
Plaça de Sant Iu
C d'En Bot
C dels Boters
Plaça Nova
Plaça de la Seu
Plaça del Rei
Jaume I
C Barra de Ferro
Hotel Banys Orientals
C dels Mirallers
La Catedral
Plaça de l'Àngel
C del Pi
C de la Palla
C del Bisbe Irurita
C de Paradís
Jaume I
C de l'Argenteria
C de la Portaferrissa
Plaça de Sant Felip Neri
Via Laietana
C del Sotstinent Navarro
C de Manresa
C de la Nau
C de Petritxol
Baixada de Sta Eulàlia
C de Sant Honorat
C de la Llibreteria
C de la Dagueria
C d'en Roca
Rambla dels Estudis
Plaça del Pi
C del Cardenal Cassañas
Plaça de St Josep Oriol
C dels Banys Nous
C del Call
C de la Ciutat
Plaça de Sant Miquel
C dels Templers
C del Cometa
C de Lledó
C del Correu Vell
C de A J Baixeras
Església de Santa Maria del Pi
C de la Boqueria
C del Palau
C de Regomir
Main Post Office
Rambla de St Josep
C d'En Rauric
C d'Avinyó
Plaça de George Orwell
C d'En Quintana
C d'En Arolas
Liceu
LA RAMBLA
C de Ferran
C de les Heures
C de la Lleona
CIUTAT VELLA
C de Cervantes
C de la Comtessa de Sobradiel
C d'Ataülf
C d'En Gignàs
C del Marquès
EL RAVAL

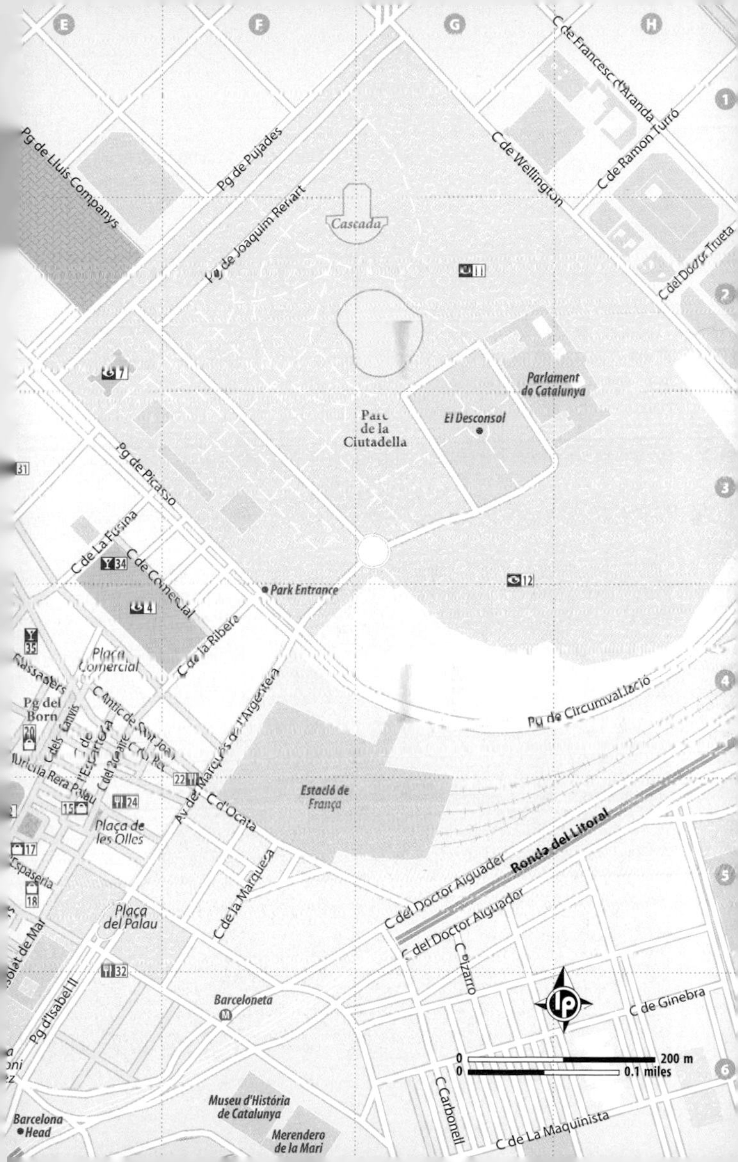

E
F
G
H
1
2
3
4
5
6
Pg de Lluís Companys
Pg de Pujades
Pg de Joaquim Renart
Cascada
C de Francesc d'Aranda
C de Wellington
C de Ramon Turró
C del Doctor Trueta
11
7
Parlament de Catalunya
El Desconsol
Parc de la Ciutadella
Pg de Picasso
31
C de La Fusina
34
C de Comercial
4
Park Entrance
12
35
Plaça Comercial
C de la Ribera
Pg del Born
20
Pg de Circumval.lació
Av del Marquès de l'Argentera
22
Estació de França
15
24
C d'Ocata
Plaça de les Olles
17
18
Ronda del Litoral
C del Doctor Aiguader
C de la Marquesa
Plaça del Palau
C del Doctor Aiguader
C Pizarro
32
Pg d'Isabel II
Barceloneta
C de Ginebra
0
200 m
0
0.1 miles
Museu d'Història de Catalunya
C Carbonell
Barcelona Head
Merendero de la Mari
C de La Maquinista

by plenty of statuary, ceramics, textiles and ritual and household objects from all over South America.

MUSEU DE LA XOCOLATA

☎ 93 268 78 78; http://pastisseria.com; Plaça de Pons i Clerch s/n; admission €3.80, free 1st Mon of month; 10am-7pm Mon & Wed-Sat, to 3pm Sun & holidays; M Jaume I; ♿

Explore the sticky story of chocolate through audiovisual displays (in English on request), touchscreen presentations, historical exhibits and the most extraordinary chocolate models of anything from grand monuments such as La Sagrada Família to cartoon characters such as Winnie the Pooh. Sign up for cooking demonstrations and tastings.

Palau de la Música Catalana

MUSEU DE ZOOLOGIA (CASTELL DELS TRES DRAGONS)

93 319 69 12; Passeig de Picasso, Parc de la Ciutadella; admission (incl Museu de Geologia) €3; 10am-2.30pm Tue, Wed & Fri-Sun, to 6.30pm Thu; M Arc de Triomf;

This rather fusty old institution is the place to seek out stuffed animals, model elephants and skeletons of huge things that lived in the past. What makes it interesting is the building itself – a whimsical 'castle' by Domènech i Montaner.

MUSEU PICASSO

93 319 63 10; www.museupicasso.bcn.es; Carrer de Montcada 15-23; adult/child under 12yr/student €6/free/3, free 1st Sun of month; 10am-8pm Tue-Sun & holidays; M Jaume I;

The setting alone, in five contiguous medieval stone mansions (p12), makes this museum worth a visit. The permanent collection, with more than 3500 pieces, is strongest on Picasso's earliest years, up until 1904. His precocious talent is clear in adolescent works such as *Retrato de la Tía Pepa* (Portrait of Aunt Pepa) and *Ciència i Caritat* (Science and Charity), both completed in 1897. There are paintings from his early Paris sojourns and then his first significant experimental stage, the Blue Period. His nocturnal blue-tinted views of *Terrats de Barcelona* (Rooftops of Barcelona) and *El Foll* (The Madman) are spectral.

MUSEU TÈXTIL I D'INDUMENTÀRIA

93 319 76 03; www.museutextil.bcn.es; Carrer de Montcada 12-14; adult/student €3.50/2 (incl Museu de les Arts Decoratives & Museu de Ceràmica), free 1st Sun of month; 10am-6pm Tue-Sat, to 3pm Sun & holidays; M Jaume I;

Fashion addicts with a sense of history will appreciate this millennia-long march-past of clobber. Inside the 13th-century mansion, you are confronted by everything from 4th-century Coptic Egyptian textiles to 20th-century local embroidery, but best is the collection that takes you through the salons of 17th-century Europe to 1930s fashion.

PALAU DE LA MÚSICA CATALANA

902 442882; www.palaumusica.org; Carrer de Sant Francesc de Paula 2; adult/child under 12yr/student incl guided tour €8/free/7; 50min tours every half-hour 10am-7pm Jul-Aug, 10am-3.30pm Sep-Jun; M Urquinaona;

The Palace of Catalan Music drips with all the fevered imagination that Modernista architect Lluís Domènech i Montaner could muster for it. Finished in 1908, its acoustics were lousy, but this World Heritage gem remains an enchanting concert setting. In 2004 a new auditorium and outdoor café were added. The exterior and foyer are opulent, but are nothing compared with the interior of the main auditorium.

PARC DE LA CIUTADELLA

Passeig de Picasso; 8am-6pm Nov-Feb, to 8pm Oct & Mar, to 9pm Apr-Sep; M Arc de Triomf;

Stroll, punt on the little lake or snooze in verdant Parc de la Ciutadella, site of Catalonia's regional parliament, the city zoo (for now; see below), a couple of museums and the monumental Cascada (waterfall) created in 1875–81 by Josep Fontsère with the help of a young Gaudí. The park was created when the hated 18th-century Ciutadella fortress, built by Madrid to keep watch over the restless population, was demolished.

ZOO DE BARCELONA

93 225 67 80; www.zoobarcelona.com; Parc de la Ciutadella; adult/child under 3yr/senior/child 3-12yr

Juggler, Parc de la Ciutadella

PERFECTLY POSITIONED?

One of the few examples of public Modernista statuary, Josep Llimona's *El Desconsol* (G3; Despair; 1906) is curiously located outside the regional Catalan parliament – a loaded political comment?

€14.95/free/7.90/9; 10am-7pm Jun-Sep, to 6pm Mar-May & Oct, to 5pm Nov-Feb; M Barceloneta;

As thrilling or depressing as any other, this small zoo occupies the southern end of the Parc de la Ciutadella and boasts 4000 creatures great and small. Plans are afoot to move the zoo to a new spot in Parc del Fòrum (p98).

SHOP

ARLEQUÍ MÀSCARES *Masks*

93 268 27 52; www.arlequimask.com; Carrer de la Princesa 7; 10.30am-8pm Mon-Sat, to 4pm Sun; M Jaume I

A little house of horrors (or delights, depending on your mood), this shop specialises in masks to wear and for decoration. Stock also includes a beautiful range of decorative boxes in Catalan themes.

CASA GISPERT *Food & Drink*

93 319 75 35; www.casagispert.com; Carrer dels Sombrerers 23; 9.30am-2pm & 4-7.30pm Tue-Fri, 10am-2pm & 5-8pm Sat; M Jaume I

Nuts and coffee are roasted in an antique, 19th-century wood-fired oven at this wonderfully aromatic wholesaler. Hazelnuts and almonds are the specialities, complemented by piles of dried fruit and a host of artisanal products, such as mustards and preserves.

CUSTO BARCELONA *Fashion*

93 268 78 93; www.custo-barcelona.com; Plaça de les Olles 7; 10am-10pm Mon-Sat; M Barceloneta

Created in the early 1980s by the Dalmau brothers, Custo is the biggest name in contemporary Barcelona fashion and one of its trendiest exports. The company

CHURCHES BURNING

Conscription of Catalans for Spain's imperialist war in Morocco lit the fuse of anarchism among disaffected workers in Barcelona in 1909. Protests spilled over into full-scale rioting against the establishment, and 70 churches, including the Església de Santa Maria del Mar (p16), were torched during what came to be known as Setmana Tràgica (Tragic Week). The anarchists attracted popular support, and when the civil war broke out in 1936 they again vented their spleen on the churches, gutting everything from La Sagrada Família (p10) to the Església de Santa Maria del Pi (p48).

Salvador Sans,
Director, Cafés El Magnífico

You've been selling coffee for a while! I'm the third Salvador Sans. We've been in this spot since 1989, but my grandfather started toasting coffee in the street in 1919. **Was that usual?** Until the 1920s, the small general store did it that way. Unfortunately I have no photos. My grandfather was auster even with photos. **And you've been importing coffee from around the world since then?** Until 1978, the state imported all coffee and distributed it. We couldn't choose and prices were fixed. **Who are your customers now?** Most of them are regular local customers. **This area (El Born) has changed a lot in the past 10 to 15 years.** It used to be awful. Tourists didr set foot here, and many Barcelonins considered it poor and run-down. The would say: You work *down there?* But I love it.

specialises in unique long-sleeved T-shirts, for men and women, with bold and psychedelic graphics. There's also a branch at **Carrer de Ferran** (Map p47, C3; ☎ 93 342 66 98; Carrer de Ferran 36).

EL MAGNÍFICO

Food & Drink

☎ 93 319 60 01, www.cafeselmagnifico.com; Carrer de l'Argenteria 64; ⏲ 9.30am-2pm & 4-8pm Mon-Fri, 9.30am-2pm Sat; Ⓜ Jaume I

Take a veritable tour of world coffee with the friendly Sans family. They had so much fun with their beans and blends that they opened another store across the street. **Sans & Sans** (D5; Carrer de l'Argenteria 59), devoted to more than 200 types of tea.

LA BOTIFARRERIA

Food & Drink

☎ 93 319 91 23; Carrer de Santa Maria 4; ⏲ 8.30am-2.30pm & 5-8.30pm Mon-Fri, 8.30am-3pm Sat; Ⓜ Jaume I

As they say, 'sausages with imagination'! Although this delightful deli sells all sorts of cheeses, hams, fresh hamburger patties, snacks and other goodies, the mainstay is an astounding variety of handcrafted sausages. Not just the pork variety, but those stuffed with anything from orange and onion to apple curry!

LA GALERÍA DE SANTA MARÍA NOVELLA

Perfumes & Herbal Remedies

☎ 93 268 02 37; www.lagaleria-smnovella.com; Carrer de l'Espaseria 4-8; ⏲ 4.30-8.30pm Mon, 10.30am-1.30pm & 4.30-8.30pm Tue-Sat; Ⓜ Jaume I

Anyone who has visited Florence may have encountered the wonderful medieval pharmacy, the Officina Profuma-Farmaceutica di Santa Maria Novella. Known for its all-natural perfumes, lotions and herbal remedies, it has become a worldwide phenomenon. How about a bottle of 'aromatic vinegar of the seven thieves'?

TALLER ANTIC

Silver & Glassware

☎ 93 310 73 03; Carrer de la Princesa 14; ⏲ 10.15am-8pm; Ⓜ Jaume I

Step back in time and place as you handle the delicate silver and glassware. Old-style perfume bottles, the kind of accessories ladies and gents might have used in the 19th century, make this a nostalgic's corner of paradise.

TOT FORMATGE

Food & Drink

☎ 93 319 53 75; Passeig del Born 13; ⏲ 5-8pm Mon, 9am-2pm & 5-8pm Tue-Fri, 10.30am-2.30pm Sat; Ⓜ Jaume I

Some gifts can certainly be a little cheesy, and none more so than the olfactory offerings in this

All Cheese locale. Little platters with samples of the products are scattered about the store. A powerful assembly of the best in Spanish and European cheeses is on display.

VILA VINITECA *Food & Drink*

☎ 93 268 32 27, 902 327777; www.vilaviniteca.es; Carrer dels Agullers 7; 8.30am-8.30pm Mon-Sat; M Jaume I
This unassuming shop has a superb range of Spanish and international wines, from cheap table varieties to vintage treasures, sold by enthusiastic staff. They know their stuff, having been in the booze business since 1932.

EAT

ÀBAC *Modern* €€€€

☎ 93 319 66 00; Carrer del Rec 79-89; lunch & dinner Tue-Sat, dinner Mon, closed Easter & Aug; M Barceloneta
This minimalist designer den continues to stun the critics. Neutral, clean lines and lighting seem deliberately conjured so as not to rob even a sliver of concentration from the imaginative dishes issuing from the kitchen. They change constantly, and might range from a tarte Tatin of eel and apple to various baby-goat offerings.

BUBÒ *Tapas* €€

☎ 93 268 72 24; Carrer de les Caputxes 10; lunch & dinner; M Jaume I; V
Pastry chef Carles Mampel operates an exquisite shop and, next door, a small restaurant where you wade through a phalanx of tapas and small savoury dishes to then get down to the serious business of trying out his devilish desserts.

CAL PEP *Tapas* €€€

☎ 93 310 79 61; Plaça de les Olles 8; dinner Mon, lunch & dinner Tue-Sat; M Barceloneta;
This boisterous tapas bar brims with energy and personality thanks to Pep, the owner and chef. Get here early for squeezing space at the bar and gourmet bar snacks, such as *cloïsses amb pernil* (clams and ham – seriously! – at €11.70). For one of the handful of tables out back, book a long way ahead.

CENTRE CULTURAL EUSKAL ETXEA *Basque* €€

☎ 93 310 21 85; Placeta de Montcada 1; lunch & dinner Tue-Sat, lunch Sun; M Jaume I;
One of the more established Basque tapas bars in Barcelona, this cultural centre still beats many of its flashier newcomer competitors for authenticity and atmosphere. Choose your *pintxos* (snacks), sip *txacoli* wine, and keep

the toothpicks so the staff can count them up and work out your bill. You could almost be in San Sebastián.

COMERÇ 24 *Modern* €€€

☎ 93 319 21 02; Carrer del Comerç 24; lunch & dinner Tue-Fri, dinner Sat; M Arc de Triomf;

In the vanguard of Barcelona's modern eateries, this place is a witches' den of almost infernal variety and extremes. The décor is unremittingly black, the cook an alumnus of local cooking guru Ferran Adriá and the cuisine eclectic. The emphasis is on waves of bite-sized snacks that traverse the culinary globe.

EL XAMPANYET *Tapas* €€

☎ 93 319 70 03; Carrer de Montcada 22; lunch & dinner Tue-Sat, lunch Sun; M Jaume I

As you emerge from the museums on this street, you might be snared by the smell of anchovies wafting out of this colourful, old-time *cava* (Spanish sparkling wine) bar, worth a visit for the setting more than the cooking.

GETTING LOST DOWN CARRER DELS BANYS VELLS

The heavy stone walls along this narrow street (D4) that runs northwest away from the Església de Santa Maria del Mar ooze centuries of history. Indeed, the street is named after the old (public) baths located here in medieval times. Various inviting restaurants, bars and shops are found here – everything from a Cuban diner to an African art shop.

HOFMANN *Mediterranean* €€€€

☎ 93 319 58 89; Carrer de l'Argenteria 74; lunch & dinner Mon-Fri; M Jaume I;

Some of the nation's great chefs learned their trade at this cooking-academy-cum-restaurant, and you won't be disappointed with the present students' efforts. An imaginative and constantly changing menu keeps chefs and diners on their toes. It's perfect for a business lunch – room should be kept for the delirium-inducing desserts.

LA FLAUTA MÁGICA *Vegetarian* €€

☎ 93 268 46 94; Carrer dels Banys Vells 18; dinner; M Jaume I; V

The menus themselves are a talking point – which album cover is yours on? *Neil Diamond Live*? *The Cars*? But on to the food. A simple burned-orange décor and low lighting set a chilled ambience for a limited menu of veggie dishes, balanced by a limited selection of dishes for carnivores, all done with free-range products.

PLA DE LA GARSA
Catalan €€

93 315 24 13; Carrer dels Assaonadors 13; dinner; M Jaume I;
This staunchly Catalan restaurant was Barcelona's hippest hang-out during the twilight of Franco's reign. Scattered with antiques and original 19th-century fixtures, the 17th-century house remains enchanting. Try the enticing *tast selecte* (tasting menu; €23.90).

SANTA MARIA *Tapas* €€€

93 315 12 27; Carrer del Comerç 17; lunch & dinner Tue-Sat; M Jaume I
Swing through the doors of this snazzy place for a smorgasbord of gourmet tapas. Beautifully decked out and always busy, Santa Maria turns out innovative and specialist creations ranging from falafel to fried plantain with mussels.

SET (7) PORTES
Catalan €€€

93 319 30 33; Passeig d'Isabel II 14; lunch & dinner; M Barceloneta;
Gilt-framed mirrors, black-and-white-tiled floors and somewhat gruff 'service' are hallmarks of this Barcelona classic, founded in 1836, once beloved of celebs and still famous for paella, seafood platters and huge portions.

DRINK

DR ASTIN *Club*

Carrer dels Abaixadors 9; 10pm-3am Thu-Sat; M Jaume I
Climb upstairs to this minuscule club setting that could be someone's badly lit lounge. DJs play a variety of electronica to a relaxed crowd.

FLOW *Bar*

93 310 06 67; Carrer de Fusina 6; 8pm-3am Tue-Sun; M Jaume I
A touched-up old-time bar, with a mirror ball and a little-used pool table, this is a curious spot for a mixed drink, where you may witness anything from experimental classical music to amateur theatre.

BAR-HOPPING ALONG PASSEIG DEL BORN

Short, leafy, cobbled Passeig del Born (E4) is the thumping heart of the nightlife that spreads out along the streets and lanes here. There's no need to single out any place along this street – they've all got a great atmosphere. Starting at the apse of Església de Santa Maria del Mar, a series of similarly good stops stretches along the left flank. Miramelindo (No 15) is a heaving barn, followed by the cosier Bermibau (No 17) with its wicker chairs and cocktails. El Copetín (No 19) and No Sé (No 21) are also good. Across the road, head upstairs at tiny Pitín (No 34).

GIMLET *Cocktail Bar*

☎ 93 310 10 27; Carrer del Rec 24; 7pm-3am; M Jaume I

Transport yourself to a Humphrey Bogart movie, almost. The punters in this timeless cocktail bar seem to get younger and grungier all the time, but the cocktails (around €7.50) remain the same, and somehow this simple little bar continues to exert a quiet magnetism.

LA FIANNA *Bar*

☎ 93 315 18 10; Carrer dels Banys Vells 15; 7pm-2am Mon-Wed, to 3am Thu-Sat, 2-11pm Sun; M Jaume I

There is something medieval-Oriental about this bar, with its bare stone walls, forged iron candelabras and cushion-covered lounges. La Fianna has another big selling point – it is one of *the* places to do Sunday brunch (from 2pm to 7pm).

LA VINYA DEL SENYOR *Wine Bar*

☎ 93 310 33 79; Plaça de Santa Maria del Mar 5; noon-1am Tue-Sun; M Jaume I

A wine-taster's fantasy, this bar has a stunning location looking out over the Església de Santa Maria del Mar. You can choose from almost 300 varieties of wine and *cava* from around the world and enjoy inventive *platillos* (mini-tapas) as you sip your drink. Try to grab the table by the window upstairs.

PALAU DE DALMASES – ESPAI BARROC *Bar*

☎ 93 310 06 73; Carrer de Montcada 20; 9pm-2am Tue-Fri, 10pm-3am Sat, 6-10pm Sun; M Jaume I

Perhaps the most pretentious bar in town, this 'baroque space' occupies the ground floor of a handsome 15th-century palace. Like a Peter Greenaway set, it is often the stage for a little light baroque music or operetta – the perfect accompaniment to your outlandishly priced goblets of wine.

PLAY

PALAU DE LA MÚSICA CATALANA *Live Music*

☎ 93 295 72 00, www.palaumusica.org; Carrer de Sant Francesc de Paula 2; admission €6-160; box office Mon-Sat 10am-9pm, 1hr before performance Sun; M Urquinaona

Aside from being a beacon of Modernisme, this multi-use venue (p79) hosts an eclectic musical programme, both in the stunning main theatre and the smaller, modern chamber-orchestra auditorium. It has a great café, too.

>PORT VELL & LA BARCELONETA

Where La Rambla meets the Med, Port Vell (Old Port) stands as pretty testimony to the city's transformation since the 1980s. You can shoot up the Columbus monument for bird's-eye views of the posh marina, World Trade Center, Maremàgnum shopping and entertainment complex and giant aquarium.

Just beyond stretches the 18th-century, working-class waterfront district of La Barceloneta. In its grid web of narrow lanes lurk countless seafood eateries. On the west side of the district bob boats in another chic marina, while the seaside beach, with its summer bars and contented buzz, is a polyglot *Who's Who* of European sun-seekers.

PORT VELL & LA BARCELONETA

SEE

Edifici de Gas Natural	1	E2
Golondrina Excursion Boats	2	B5
L'Aquàrium	3	D4
Monument a Colom	4	B5
Museu d'Història de Catalunya	5	D3
Museu Marítim	6	A5
Transbordador Aeri	7	B6

EAT

El Vaso de Oro	8	D2
Suquet de l'Almirall	9	E4
Torre d'Alta Mar	10	D5

DRINK

Daguiri	11	E4
Sugar Club	12	C6

PLAY

Club Natació Atlètic-Barcelona	13	E6
Poliesportiu Marítim	14	F1

Please see over for map

SEE

EDIFICI DE GAS NATURAL

Passeig de Salvat Papasseit, La Barceloneta; M Barceloneta

While only 100m high, this brand-new shimmering glass waterfront tower – designed by Enric Miralles – is extraordinary for its mirrorlike surface and weirdly protruding adjunct buildings, which could be giant glass cliffs bursting from the main tower's flank.

GOLONDRINA EXCURSION BOATS

☎ 93 442 31 06; www.lasgolondrinas.com; Moll de les Drassanes, Port Vell; adult/child under 4yr/child aged 4-10yr €7.50/free/2; several outings daily; M Drassanes

Kids will love the 1½-hour jaunt around the harbour and along the beaches to the northeast tip of town aboard a *golondrina* (swallow). Shorter trips are also available (and tend to leave more often).

L'AQUÀRIUM

☎ 93 221 74 74; www.aquariumbcn.com; Moll d'Espanya, Port Vell; adult/child under 4yr/child 4-12yr/senior over 60yr €15/free/10/12; 9.30am-11pm Jul & Aug, to 9.30pm Jun & Sep, to 9pm Mon-Fri, to 9.30pm Sat & Sun Oct-May; M Drassanes

You won't come much closer to a set of shark choppers. The

BEACHED BOXES

American Rebecca Horn's striking tribute to La Barceloneta, *Homenatge a la Barceloneta* (F4) is an eye-catching column of rusted iron and glass cubes on Platja de Sant Sebastià.

A
B
C
D
1
2
3
4
5
6
LA RIBERA
C de Ripoll
Plaça Antoni Maura
C de Colomines
C de la Princesa
C del Rec
C de Comercial
Plaça Comercial
C de Montcada
Pg del Born
Plaça de R Berenguer Gran
Jaume I
BARRI GÒTIC
Plaça de la Seu
Plaça de Sant Iu
C dels Mirallers
C dels Canvis
C del Bonaire
Estació de França
Plaça de les Olles
Jaume I
Plaça de Sta Maria del Mar
Plaça de Sant Felip Neri
Plaça de Sant Josep Oriol
Plaça de Sant Jaume
Plaça del Palau
Plaça de Sant Miquel
Pg d'Isabel II
Barceloneta
Plaça del Pau Vila
Liceu
C de Ferran
CIUTAT VELLA
C d'Ataülf
Plaça d'Antoni López
5
Palau de Mar
Barcelona Head
Moll del Dipòsit
LA RAMBLA
C dels Escudellers
C d'Avinyó
C d'En Serra
C del Còdols
Mirador del Port Vell
Plaça de la Mercè
Moll d'Espanya
Moll de la Barcel
EL RAVAL
Plaça del Teatre
Plaça de Joaquim Xirau
Plaça del Duc de Medinaceli
Marina
Pg de Colom
Ronda del Litoral
Moll de la Fusta
Pailebot de Santa Eulàlia
Drassanes
3
Av de les Drassanes
Plaça del Portal de la Pau
4
PORT VELL
6
Pg de Josep Carner
Moll de les Drassanes
2
Maremàgnum
Moll d'Espanya
Port de Barcelona
Moll de Balears
C de Vila i Vilà
Moll de Barcelona
7
Torre Sant Seb
Pg de Josep
World Trade Center
12
Moll de Sant Bertran
Port Vell

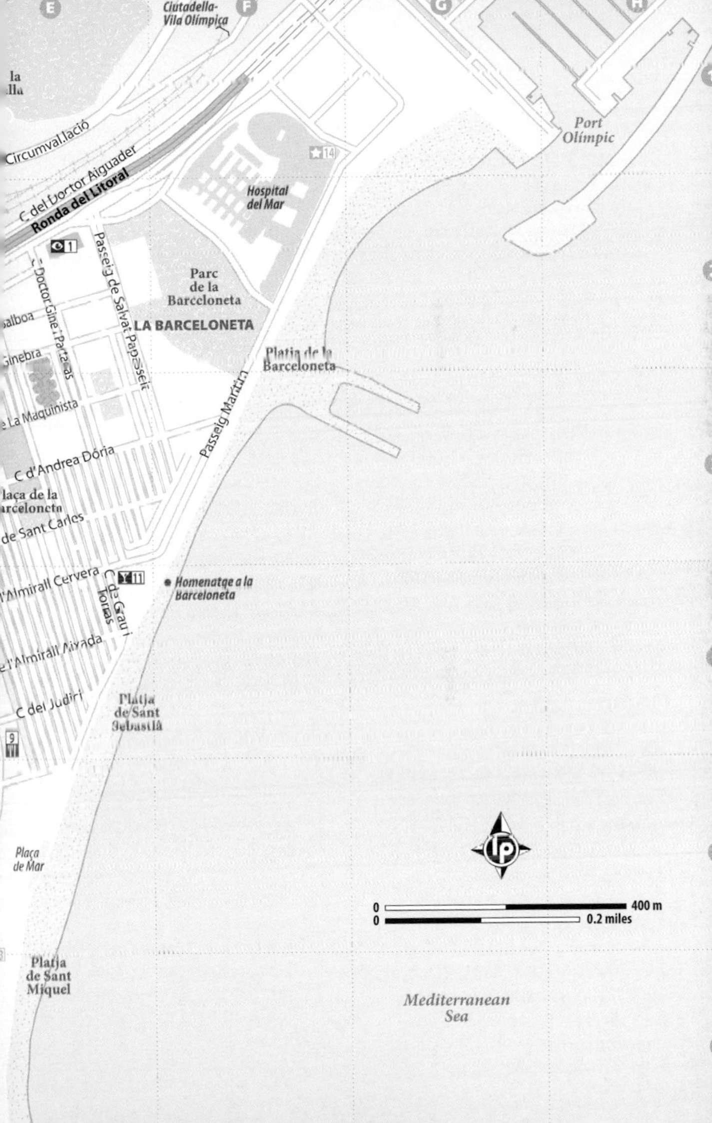

E
F
G
H
Ciutadella-Vila Olímpica
Circumval.lació
C del Doctor Aiguader
Ronda del Litoral
Port Olímpic
Hospital del Mar
14
1
Parc de la Barceloneta
LA BARCELONETA
Passeig de Salvat Papasseit
C Doctor Giné i Partagàs
Platja de la Barceloneta
Passeig Marítim
C de La Maquinista
C d'Andrea Dòria
Plaça de la Barceloneta
C de Sant Carles
C de l'Almirall Cervera
C de Grau i Torras
11
Homenatge a la Barceloneta
C de l'Almirall Aixada
C del Judici
Platja de Sant Sebastià
9
Plaça de Mar
Platja de Sant Miquel
Mediterranean Sea
0
400 m
0
0.2 miles
1
2
3
4
5
6

PORTSIDE MEANDER ALONG PASSEIG DE JOAN DE BORBÓ

Maybe it's a good thing the Metro doesn't reach the beach at La Barceloneta, obliging you to walk down the sunny portside promenade of Passeig de Joan de Borbó (D4). Megayachts sway gently on your right as you bowl down a street crackling with activity. Folks chomp cheerfully at pavement terraces, with eateries ranging from kebab stands to century-old seafood joints. King of the lot is Suquet de l'Almirall (p94). In among them you'll pass a popular Irish pub, the Fastnet (No 22), a couple of ice-cream shops, three shoe stores, a squat (No 10) and a small supermarket for beach supplies.

80m-long shark tunnel is the high point in this, one of Europe's largest aquariums. Some 11,000 fish (including about a dozen sharks) have become permanent residents here in an area filled with 4.5 million litres of water. The restless sharks are accompanied by splendid flapping rays and huge sunfish. Other tanks are devoted to the delights of the Red Sea, the Caribbean, Hawaii, Australia and the South Seas.

MONUMENT A COLOM

☎ 93 302 52 24; Plaça del Portal de la Pau, Port Vell; lift adult/child under 4 yr/senior & child 4-12yr €2.30/free/1.50; 9am-8.30pm May-Oct, 10am-6.30pm Nov-Apr; M Drassanes

Centuries after he stumbled across the Americas, Columbus was honoured with this 60m monument, built for the Universal Exhibition in 1888. It looks like he's urging the tourists to go elsewhere, but you can catch a lift to the soles of his feet for a fine view.

MUSEU D'HISTÒRIA DE CATALUNYA

☎ 93 225 47 00; www.mhcat.net; Plaça de Pau Vila 3, Port Vell; admission €3, free 1st Sun of month; 10am-7pm Tue & Thu-Sat, to 8pm Wed, to 2.30pm Sun & holidays; M Barceloneta;

From the caves of the Pyrenees to air-raid shelters of the civil war, see how Catalans and other folk (including Romans and Arabs) have rolled with history's ups and

ART POPS UP IN PORT VELL

Designed by the American pop artist Roy Lichtenstein in 1992, the 14m *Barcelona Head* (C3) sculpture, just back from Port Vell at the end of Passeig de Colom, sparkles like a ceramic comic when the sun strikes its broken-tile coating, believed to be a homage to Gaudí.

downs over 2000 years in this hectic but entertaining interactive display. Pick up a guide in English at reception and don't miss the view from the top-floor restaurant.

MUSEU MARÍTIM

93 342 99 20; www.museumaritim barcelona.org; Avinguda de les Drassanes, Port Vell; admission €6, free 3-8pm 1st Sat of month; 10am-8pm; M Drassanes;

Much of Barcelona's medieval prosperity depended on sea trade. In these one-time Gothic shipyards, you can get a sense of the glory and adventure of centuries of maritime history (see p24), from the era of rafts to the age of steam. Entry also gives access to the 1918 three-master *Pailebot de Santa Eulàlia*, moored at Port Vell (C4).

TRANSBORDADOR AERI

Passeig Escullera, La Barceloneta; one way/return €7.50/9; 11am-8pm mid-Jun–mid-Sep, 10.45am-7pm Mar–mid-Jun & mid-Sep–late Oct, 10am-6pm late Oct-Feb; M Barceloneta, 17, 39 & 64

This cable car (aka *funicular aeri*), strung out precariously across the

Transbordador Aeri

harbour to Montjuïc, provides a bird's-eye view of the city. The cabins float between Miramar (Montjuïc) and the Torre de Sant Sebastià (La Barceloneta).

EAT

EL VASO DE ORO *Tapas* €€

93 319 30 98; Carrer de Balboa 6, La Barceloneta; 11am-midnight; M Barceloneta;

If you like noisy, crowded bars, high-speed bar staff always ready with a smile and a wise-crack, a cornucopia of tapas and the illusion, in here at least, that Barcelona hasn't changed in decades, come to the sassy 'Glass of Gold' on the edge of La Barceloneta.

SUQUET DE L'ALMIRALL

Seafood €€€

93 221 62 33; Passeig de Joan de Borbó 65, La Barceloneta; lunch & dinner Tue-Sat, lunch Sun; 17, 39, 57 & 64;

The order of the day here is simply top-class seafood. House specialities include *arròs a la barca* (rice laden with various types of fish, squid and tomato) or *suquet* (seafood stew). There are plenty of seafood eateries offering a wide variety tucked away in nearby lanes.

TORRE D'ALTA MAR

Mediterranean €€€€

93 221 00 07; Torre de Sant Sebastià, Passeig de Joan de Borbó 88, La Barceloneta; lunch & dinner Tue-Sat, lunch Mon; 17, 39, 57 & 64;

The people of Barcelona are known for their fickleness, and this towering restaurant fell out of favour just as quickly as it had fallen in. Nothing can alter the fact, however, that the aerial views from the top of this metal tower remain the most spectacular dining setting in the whole town. Seafood dominates, the wine list is strong and the food and service are generally good as well.

DRINK

DAGUIRI *Bar*

93 221 51 09; Carrer de Grau i Torras 59, La Barceloneta; 10am-1.30am Wed-Mon; M Barceloneta

This take-it-easy, seaside bar was made for its young, travelling crowd – the kind who have elected to hang out in Barcelona for a stretch in search of themselves or until their pennies run out. Have a light meal, sip a summertime beer outside or cosy up for a coffee in winter at the tiny tables inside.

SEAFOOD AT THE PALAU DE MAR

The beautifully restored portside warehouses of the Palau de Mar (D3) are not just home to the intriguing Museu d'Història de Catalunya (p92). Facing the bobbing yachts is a series of five seafood restaurants, all with sunny terraces. Prices range from €35 to €40 per head and locals change their minds constantly about which (if any) are worthy of their custom, but there are few more pleasant spots to peel prawns – except, of course, in the museum café-restaurant at the top of the building.

SUGAR CLUB

Restaurant-Club

☎ 93 508 83 2[illegible]; www.sugarclub-barcelona.com; World Trade Center, Moll de Barcelona, Port Vell; 11pm-3am Wed-Sat; M Drassanes

Head to this dapper restaurant-club with DJ play anything from contemporary pop-rock to house and a snappily dressed crowd. The food is fusion funky and skipped without remorse, but the music served up can be top class, with such local DJs at the turntables as David Mas.

PLAY

CLUB NATACIÓ ATLÈTIC-BARCELONA *Swimming*

☎ 93 221 00 10; www.cnab.org; Plaça de Mar s/n, La Barceloneta; adult/child up to 10yr €9.50/5.70; 6.30am-11pm Mon-Fri, 7am-11pm Sat year-round, 8am-5pm Sun & holidays Oct–mid-May, 8am-8pm Sun & holidays mid-May–Sep; 17, 39, 57 & 64;

Down near La Barceloneta beach, this athletic club has one indoor and two outdoor pools. Of the outdoor offerings, one is heated for lap swimming during winter. The admission charge includes use of the gym and private beach access.

POLIESPORTIU MARÍTIM

Swimming & Thalassotherapy

☎ 93 224 04 40; www.claror.org/maritim.htm; Passeig Marítim 33-35, La Barceloneta; admission Mon-Fri €13.50, Sat, Sun & holidays €16; 7am-midnight Mon-Fri, 8am-9pm Sat, 8am-4pm Sun & holidays; M Ciutadella-Vila Olímpica;

Water babies will squeal with delight in this thalassotherapeutic (sea-water therapy) sports centre. Apart from the smallish swimming pool, there is a labyrinth of hot, warm and freezing-cold spa pools, along with thundering waterfalls that are wonderful for some massage relief.

>PORT OLÍMPIC, POBLENOU & EL FÒRUM

Strolling, skating or riding your bicycle northeast from La Barceloneta, you'll reach Port Olímpic, a crammed marina that was created for the 1992 Olympics. It is lined by heaving if largely tacky bars and eateries. Barcelona's classiest hotel stands here, too.

More beaches spread northeast towards an impressive development project. Amid the high-rise apartments and luxury hotels lies Parc del Fòrum. Dominated by the weird, triangular Edifici Fòrum, an enormous conference centre and huge photovoltaic panel, it comes to life in summer with a protected bathing area, marina, kids' playgrounds, concerts and a temporary disco. The zoo will one day move here too.

PORT OLÍMPIC, POBLENOU & EL FÒRUM

SEE

Museu de Carrosses Fúnebres........1 A3
Torre Agbar........2 A2

EAT

Els Pescadors........3 D3

DRINK

CDLC........4 B6

PLAY

Baja Beach Club........5 C6
Casino........6 C6
Icària Yelmo Cineplex...7 C5
Razzmatazz........8 B3

A
B
C
D
Parc del Clot
C Escultors Claperós
Gran Via de les Corts Catalanes
SANT MARTÍ
Av Diagonal
To El Maresme Fòrum Station (500m); Parc de Fòrum (700m)
C de Bac de Roda
0
400 m
0
0.2 miles
Glòries
2
C de Roc Boronat
C de Pere IV
C de Pallars
El Poblenou
C de Ciutat de Granada
EL POBLENOU
Rambla del Poblenou
C de Bolívia
C de Badajoz
C de Tànger
C de Àvila
Llacuna
C dels Almogàvers
C de Ramon Turró
Av Meridiana
8
3
C de Zamora
C de Pere IV
C de Llull
C de Jaume Vicens i Vives
C del Doctor Trueta
To Parc del Fòrum (2km)
1
C de Pallars
C de Pamplona
Marina
C de Arquitecte Sert
C de Ramon Turró
Bogatell
C de Sancho d'Àvila
C de Joan Oliver
C de Llull
C de Frederic Mompou
Pg de Pujades
Av del Bogatell
C de Sardenya
C de la Marina
VILA OLÍMPICA
7
Platja de Bogatell
Pg Marítim de Nova Icària
C de Wellington
Av d'Icària
C de Salvador Espriu
Platja de la Nova Icària
Parc de la Ciutadella
C de Francesc d'Aranda
Pg Marítim del Port Olímpic
Parlament de Catalunya
C de Vilena
Plaça dels Voluntaris Olímpics
C de Moscou
Ciutadella-Vila Olímpica
David i Goliat
C de la Marina
6
C del Doctor Aiguader
C de Torrevieja
Pg Marítim de la Barceloneta
C de Trelawny
Pg de Circumval·lació
Ronda del Litoral
4
Hospital del Mar
5
Port Olímpic

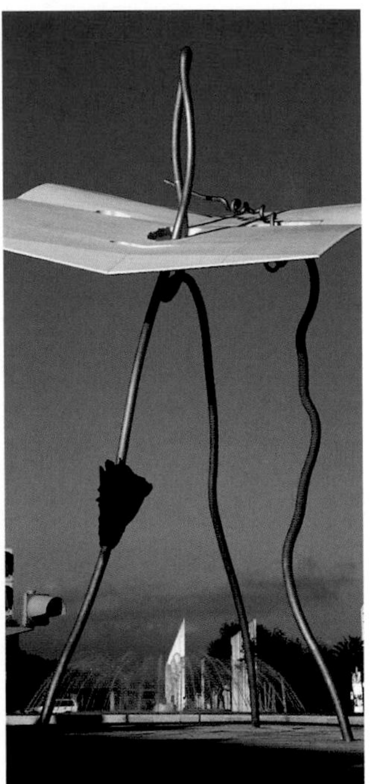

THEY MIGHT BE GIANTS

In the shadow of the two skyscrapers of the Vila Olímpica (Olympic village) on Plaça dels Voluntaris Olímpics, Antoni Llena's 1993 sculpture *David i Goliat* (B6) honours the poor who were uprooted from this neighbourhood. It consists of a large metal sheet shaped like a mask and suspended 20m up on three steel tubes.

SEE

PARC DEL FÒRUM

☎ 93 356 10 50; www.bcn.es/parcdelforum; Rambla de Prim 2-4, El Fòrum; Ⓜ El Maresme Fòrum; Ⓟ ♿
Once a wasteland around a creaky sewerage plant, the Parc del Fòrum lies at the heart of an ambitious urban-renewal project. The Edifici Fòrum houses a permanent exhibition on Barcelona's urban transformation, **Barcelona Propera** (admission free; 🕒 11am-8pm Tue-Sun). The highlight is an amazingly detailed 1:1000 scale model of the city. It took 20,000 man-hours (more than five months) to create and is claimed to be the biggest such city model in Europe. The **Zona de Banys** (🕒 11am-8pm May-Sep) bathing area has kayaks and bikes for rent, and even the chance to learn to dive.

TORRE AGBAR

www.torreagbar.com; Avinguda Diagonal 225, Poblenou; Ⓜ Glòries
Barcelona's very own cucumber-shaped tower, Jean Nouvel's luminous Torre Agbar (headquarters of the city water company) is the most daring addition to Barcelona's skyline since the first towers of La Sagrada Família went up. Completed in 2005, it shimmers in shades of midnight blue and lipstick red, especially at night. You can wander into the foyer.

EAT

ELS PESCADORS

Seafood €€€

☎ **93 225 20 18; www.elspescadors.com; Plaça de Prim 1, Poblenou; lunch & dinner; M Poblenou;**

Fresh fish brought down from coastal fish markets dominates the menu at this pleasing restaurant on a quiet square. Oven-baked catch of the day and gourmet cod dishes are strong cards. Eat outside or in the timber-lined interior, whose timeless tavern atmosphere has been maintained.

Torre Aqbar

SPOILT FOR CHOICE

Classic movies are sometimes shown in such diverse locations as La Pedrera (p109), Sala Apolo (p151), FNAC record and book store in the El Triangle shopping centre on Plaça de Catalunya (p115), CaixaForum (p143) and the Centre de Cultura Contemporània de Barcelona (p66). Summer screens are set up by the pool at Piscines Bernat Picornell (p150) and in the Parc del Fòrum (p98), too.

CaixaForum cinema complex

DRINK

CDLC *Club*

☎ 93 224 04 70; www.cdlcbarcelona.com; Passeig Marítim de la Barceloneta 32, La Barceloneta; 10am-3am; M Ciutadella-Vila Olímpica

The Carpe Diem Lounge Club is one of the hippest locales on Barcelona's waterfront. Stretch out on the 'Bali' lounges, get mysterious in the Morocco space, dance away inside or sip cocktails outside to an acoustic diet of chill while gazing over the sand and sea. What's more, you can feel just as cool here for breakfast, lunch and dinner (the kitchen closes and tables are cleared from the dance floor at midnight).

PLAY

BAJA BEACH CLUB *Club*

☎ 93 225 91 00; www.bajabeach.es; Passeig Marítim 34; 1pm-5am Sun-Thu, to 6am Fri & Sat; M Ciutadella-Villa Olímpica

Go-go girls and boys, thundering dance music, bleary eyes – this club is an unabashed, unpretentious seaside dancing and pick-up joint. All good fun really and with a high component of out-of-towners among the mostly unsteady punters. In the afternoon it's not a bad spot for a beer overlooking the beach.

CASINO

☎ 93 225 78 78; www.casino-barcelona.com; Carrer de la Marina 19-21; admission €4.50; 11am-5am; M Ciutadella-Vila Olímpica

Feeling lucky? If this is your night, you might manage to walk out of here with some extra cash for a bottle of *cava* in one of the nearby bars and clubs.

ICÀRIA YELMO CINEPLEX *Cinema*

☎ 93 221 75 85; www.yelmocineplex.es; Carrer de Salvador Espriu 61, VIla Olímpica; admission €5.80-6.50; up to 6 sessions 11am-10.30pm, plus movie after midnight Fri & Sat; M Ciutadella-Vila Olímpica;

Behind the Port Olímpic, this multiplex has 15 screens showing mainstream and art-house movies in the original language – the biggest such concentration in the city.

RAZZMATAZZ *Club*

☎ 93 272 09 10; www.salarazzmatazz.com; Carrer dels Almogàvers 122 or Carrer de Pamplona 88; admission €10-25; 1am-6am Fri & Sat; M Marina

Five clubs are crammed into one huge warehouse space to make this one of the most popular dance destinations in town. You can enjoy anything from rock and indie to garage, techno and '60s nostalgia. Headline acts also perform here regularly.

>L'EIXAMPLE

By far the most extensive of Barcelona's districts, this sprawling grid is full of sub-identities. Almost all the city's Modernista buildings were raised in L'Eixample. The pick of them line Passeig de Gràcia, but hundreds adorn the area. Work on Gaudí's La Sagrada Família church continues.

L'EIXAMPLE

SEE

Casa Batlló 1 D4
Casa Calvet 2 E4
Casa de les Punxes (Casa Terrades)..............3 D2
Fundació Antoni Tàpies...4 D4
Fundación Francisco Godia 5 D4
La Pedrera (Casa Milà)...6 C3
La Sagrada Família........7 E1
Manzana de la Discordia 8 D4
Museu de Carrosses Fúnebres........................9 H3
Museu del Perfum.......10 D4
Museu Egipci 11 D4
Palau del Baró Quadras (Casa Asia)..................12 C3

SHOP

Adolfo Domínguez......13 D4
Altäir 14 D5
Antonio Miró 15 D4
Armand Basi................16 D4
Bad Habits...................17 D3
Bulevard dels Antiquaris...................18 D4
Bulevard Rosa 19 D4
Camper........................20 C4
Casa del Llibre.............21 D4
El Corte Inglés 22 E5
Els Encants Vells......... 23 G1
Farrutx........................24 C3
Favorita 25 D3
Floristería Navarro 26 D3
FNAC...........................27 D5
Joan Murrià 28 D3
Joaquín Berao 29 C4
Josep Font 30 D3
Laie.............................31 E4
Loewe.........................32 D4
Mango 33 C4
Marc 3......................... 34 D5
Mas Bacus....................35 C4
Norma Comics.............36 F4
Roser-Francesc............37 D3
Sephora.......................38 D5
Vinçon 39 C3
Zara 40 E4

EAT

Alba Granados.............41 C5
Alkímia 42 E1
Amaltea...................... 43 C6
Casa Calvet ....(see 2)
Casa Darío 44 C5
Cata 1.81 ....45 C5
Cerveseria Catalana ... 46 C4
Dolso 47 C4
Mauri 48 C3
Patagonia....................49 E4
Saüc............................50 A4
Sense Pressa................51 B4
Speakeasy 52 B4
Taktika Berri................53 C5
Thai Gardens 54 D4

DRINK

Aire.............................55 C4
Buda Barcelona 56 E4
Dietrich Gay Teatro Café 57 C5
Distrito Diagonal........ 58 C3
Dry Martini..................59 B4
Hotel Omm Bar........... 60 C3
Les Gens Que J'Aime....61 D3
Michael Collins Pub.... 62 E2
Sweet Café 63 C5

PLAY

Antilla BCN 64 B6
Arena Madre................65 D5
L'Auditori 66 G2
Masajes a 1000............67 C4
Metro......................... 68 D6
New Chaps...................69 C3
Plaça de Braus Monumental Bullring...........70 G2
Renoir Floridablanca...71 C6
Salvation 72 E4
Teatre Nacional de Catalunya 73 G2

Please see over for map

Shoppers converge on Passeig de Gràcia and La Rambla de Catalunya. At night, mainly Thursday to Saturday, Carrer d'Aribau and nearby streets pound with nightlife as local punters let their hair down. The 'Gaixample', around Carrer del Consell de Cent and Carrer de Muntaner, is a pole of gay nightlife. Restaurants of all possible shades and shapes are scattered across the district.

SEE

CASA BATLLÒ

93 216 03 06; www.casabatllo.es; Passeig de Gràcia 43; adult/student & senior €16.50/13; 9am-8pm; M Passeig de Gràcia

One of the weirdest-looking concoctions to emerge from the fantastical imagination of Antoni Gaudí is this apartment block, which he renovated early in the 20th century. Locals know it as the *casa dels ossos* (house of bones) or *casa del drac* (house of the dragon) and it's not hard to see why. The balconies look like the jaws of some strange beast and the roof represents Sant Jordi (St George) and the dragon. The staircase wafts you up to the 1st floor, where everything swirls in the main salon: the ceiling is twisted into a vortex around its sunlike lamp; the doors, window and skylights are dreamy waves of wood and coloured glass. The same themes continue in the other rooms and covered terrace. Twisting, tiled chimney pots add a surreal touch to the roof.

Window detail, Casa Batllò

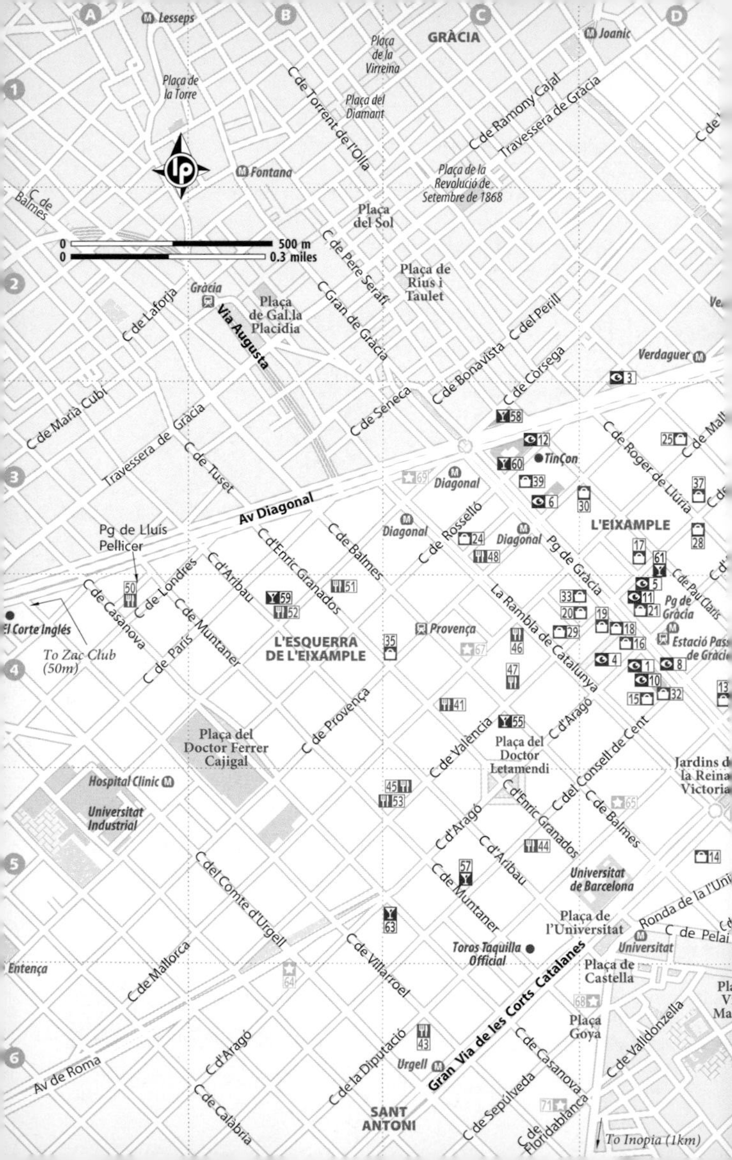

Lesseps
GRÀCIA
Joanic
Plaça de la Virreina
Plaça de la Torre
Plaça del Diamant
C de Torrent de l'Olla
C de Ramon y Cajal
Travessera de Gràcia
Fontana
Plaça de la Revolució de Setembre de 1868
C de Balmes
Plaça del Sol
0 500 m
0 0.3 miles
C de Pere Serafí
Plaça de Rius i Taulet
Gràcia
Plaça de Gal.la Placidia
C de Laforja
Via Augusta
C Gran de Gràcia
C del Perill
Verdaguer
C de Bonavista
C de Còrsega
C de Seneca
C de Maria Cubí
Travessera de Gràcia
C de Tuset
C de Roger de Llúria
TinÇon
Diagonal
Av Diagonal
L'EIXAMPLE
Pg de Lluís Pellicer
C d'Enric Granados
C de Balmes
C de Rosselló
Pg de Gràcia
C de Pau Claris
C de Londres
C d'Aribau
La Rambla de Catalunya
C de Casanova
C de Muntaner
El Corte Inglés
To Zac Club (50m)
C de París
L'ESQUERRA DE L'EIXAMPLE
Provença
Estació Passeig de Gràcia
C de Provença
C d'Aragó
C de València
Plaça del Doctor Ferrer Cajigal
Plaça del Doctor Letamendi
C del Consell de Cent
Jardins de la Reina Victoria
Hospital Clínic
Universitat Industrial
C d'Enric Granados
C de Balmes
C d'Aragó
C d'Aribau
C del Comte d'Urgell
C de Muntaner
Universitat de Barcelona
Plaça de l'Universitat
Ronda de la Universitat
C de Pelai
C de Villarroel
Toros Taquilla Official
Universitat
Entença
C de Mallorca
Plaça de Castella
Gran Via de les Corts Catalanes
Plaça Goya
C de Valldonzella
C d'Aragó
C de la Diputació
C de Casanova
Av de Roma
Urgell
C de Sepúlveda
C de Calàbria
SANT ANTONI
C de Floridablanca
To Inopia (1km)

E
F
G
H
1
2
3
4
5
6
To Hospital de la Santa Creu i Sant Pau (500m)
Av de Gaudí
C de Lepant
Plaça de Gaudí
Sagrada Família
SAGRADA FAMÍLIA
7
Plaça de la Sagrada Família
62
C de Sicília
C de València
C d'Aragó
C del Consell de Cent
C del Dos de Maig
23
Plaça de les Glòries Catalanes
Glòries
C de Mallorca
Av Diagonal
Plaça de Braus Monumental
70
73
Plaça de les Arts
C de Lepant
Monumental
66
C de la Marina
C d'Aragó
C del Consell de Cent
Pg de Sant Joan
C de Sardenya
C de Sicília
Av Meridiana
C de Sancho d'Àvila
9
C de Bailèn
Tetuan
Marina
Bogatell
C de Girona
Girona
EL FORT PIUS
C de la Diputació
Gran Via de les Corts Catalanes
C d'Ausiàs Marc
Plaça Mossén Jacint Verdaguer
36
Arc de Triomf
C del Bruc
C de Francesc d'Aranda
49
56
2
C de Casp
Pg de Pujades
Arc de Triomf
Plaça del Comerç
Pg de Joaquim Pena
Parc de la Ciutadella
C de Wellington
Urquinaona
Plaça de Sant Pere
C Comtal
Ronda de Sant Pere
Urquinaona
C d'Ortigosa
22
C de Fontanella
C del Comerç
Plaça Tetuan
Av del Portal de l'Àngel
C de Ripoll
LA RIBERA
C de la Princesa
C Comercial
Plaça de Ramon Amadeu
Plaça Antoni Maura
C dels Corders
C de Jaume I
Pg del Born
Plaça Comercial
Pg de Circumval.lació
Plaça de la Seu
Plaça de l'Àngel
Jaume I
BARRI GÒTIC
LA RAMBLA
Rambla de Canaletes
Jaume I
Ronda del Litoral
Plaça de Sant Jaume
Via Laietana
Plaça del Palau
Plaça de Sant Miquel
CIUTAT VELLA
Pg d'Isabel II
EL RAVAL
LA BARCELONETA
Barceloneta
Plaça d'Antoni Lopez
Plaça de la Gardunya
Liceu

CASA CALVET

☎ 93 412 40 12; Carrer de Casp 48; Ⓜ Urquinaona

Gaudí's first apartment block and most conventional building won him the only award of his life – the city council's prize for the best building of 1900. Sober from the outside, there are hints of whimsy in the ground-floor restaurant.

CASA DE LES PUNXES

Avinguda Diagonal 420; Ⓜ Diagonal

Puig i Cadafalch could have been eating too much cheese late at

Fundació Antoni Tàpies

ight when he created this neo-Gothic fantasy, built between 1903 and 1905. Officially the Casa Terrades, the building's pointed turrets earned it the nickname Casa de les Punxes (House of Spikes).

FUNDACIÓ ANTONI TÀPIES

☎ 93 487 03 15; www.fundaciotapies.org; Carrer d'Aragó 255; adult/student €4.20/2.10; 10am-8pm Tue-Sun; M Passeig de Gràcia;

This Domènech i Montaner building – considered by many to be the prototype for Modernisme, and the first in the city to be built on an iron frame – houses the experimental work of Catalonia's greatest living artist, Antoni Tàpies, as well as exhibitions by other contemporary artists. The building is crowned with coiled wire, a curious Tàpies sculpture titled *Núvol i Cadira* (Cloud and Chair).

FUNDACIÓN FRANCISCO GODIA

☎ 93 272 31 80; www.fundacionfgodia.org; Carrer de València 284; adult/child under 5yr/student & senior €4.50/free/2.10; 10am-8pm Wed-Mon; M Passeig de Gràcia;

An intriguing mix of medieval art, ceramics and modern paintings makes up this eclectic private collection. Medieval works include wooden sculptures of the Virgin Mary and Christ taken down from the Cross, and there are paintings by such Catalan icons as Jaume Huguet and Valencia's Joaquim Sorolla.

HOSPITAL DE LA SANTA CREU I DE SANT PAU

☎ 902 076621; www.santpau.es; Carrer de Cartagena; guided tour €5; tours 10.15am & 12.15pm in English, 11.15am in Catalan, 1.15pm in Spanish; M Hospital de Sant Pau;

A Domènech i Montaner masterpiece, begun in 1901 and finished

MODERNISME UNPACKED

Modernisme aficionados should consider the *Ruta del Modernisme* pack (€12). You receive a guide to 115 buildings, a map and discounts (valid for a year) of up to 50% on the main Modernista sights in Barcelona, as well as some elsewhere in Catalonia. For €18, you get another guide and map, *Sortim,* which leads you to bars and restaurants in Modernista buildings. The packs are available at three Centres del Modernisme and the books alone at bookshops. For more information call ☎ 902 076621 or ☎ 93 317 76 52 or check out the website (www.rutadelmodernisme.com).

Lluís Bosch,

Publishing Head of the Barcelona Urban Landscape Institute

Years ago, Gaudí's La Pedrera was a blackened block of flats. People thought it was horrible; now it's the most famous house in Barcelona. **Gaud was the best thing to ever happen to Barcelona!** Undoubtedly! The FC Ba celona museum was Barcelona's top attraction 15 years ago. Now architectu is the main draw. **So it's not just stag nights?** Ha ha! That's a more recent trend. **What's your favourite Modernista building?** Casa Macaya. A beauti house by Puig i Cadafalch. **Aside from Modernisme, what else gives you a chitectural pleasure?** The medieval city, especially where the Roman city w **Where do you go for fun?** The Old City or Gràcia. I prefer smaller bars, like Ascensor and Harlem, a quaint jazz place. In Gràcia, Bar Maria is good. **Woulc you live anywhere else?** Yes, but eventually I would come back to Barcelon y his son in 1930, this uniquely chirpy hospital is a gargantuan Modernista landmark comprising 18 lavishly decorated pavilions. Feign illness or just wander around the gardens. The hospital wards are being transferred to more modern facilities, and the site will eventually house a museum on medicine and Montaner.

LA PEDRERA

☎ 902 400973; www.fundaciocaixa catalunya.es; Carrer de Provença 261-265; adult/student & EU senior €8/4.50; 🕑 10am-8pm; Ⓜ Diagonal; ♿

The most extraordinary apartment block built in Barcelona was actually called Casa Milà – after its owner – but nicknamed La Pedrera (the Stone Quarry) by bemused locals who watched Antoni Gaudí build it from 1905 to 1910. Its rippling grey stone façade looks like a cliff face sculpted by waves and wind. It is studded with 'seaweed' in the form of wrought-iron balconies. On the 4th floor, visit a re-created Modernista apartment, El Pis de la Pedrera, furnished in the style a prosperous family might have enjoyed when the block was completed. The Espai Gaudí (Gaudí Space) is housed in what used to be the attic and feels like the building's ribcage. It now offers an overview of Gaudí's work. The roof is adorned with what look like giant medieval (or 21st-century!) knights. They are in fact hallucinatory chimneypots. La Pedrera also occasionally hosts live music and films – call for details.

LA SAGRADA FAMÍLIA

☎ 93 207 30 31; www.sagradafamilia .org; Carrer de Mallorca 401; adult/student €8/5, combined with Casa Museu Gaudí in Park Güell €9; 🕑 9am-8pm Apr-Sep, to 6pm Oct-Mar; Ⓜ Sagrada Família; ♿

Antoni Gaudí's most extraordinary creation, still years from completion, is an everchanging magnet for visitors. Gaudí started work

THE CALM OF CARRER D'ENRIC GRANADOS

Half the city's population would like to live here. Mr Granados (1867–1916), a classical musician, probably wouldn't have minded either. The pedestrianised bottom end, at Carrer de la Diputació, is marked off by the **gardens** (D5; 🕑 10am-sunset Sat & Sun from Carrer de la Diputació, 10am-sunset Mon-Fri from Plaça de l'Universitat) of the Universitat de Barcelona. The banter of diners can be heard at a couple of nearby restaurants as you wander between rows of elegant apartments to the leafy (but noisy) Plaça del Doctor Letamendi (C5). From here on, one lane of traffic trickles down the rest of the street, along which are stationed more tempting eateries until you reach Avinguda Diagonal.

on La Sagrada Família (see also p10) in 1884. The Nativity façade was finished in 1935, nine years after his death. The following year, anarchists destroyed many of his plans. Work restarted in 1952 and the Passion façade was raised in 1976. The finishing touches to its décor, with bold, angular and highly controversial work depicting the passion and death of Christ by sculptor Josep Maria Subirachs, are being carried out now. In the crypt is a museum bursting with models, photographs and other material on the building's history. When finished, the enormous temple will have room for 13,000 faithful – the problem may be finding that many faithful.

MANZANA DE LA DISCORDIA

Passeig de Gràcia; Ⓜ Passeig de Gràcia
One might be tempted to believe some wiseacre in the Barcelona

WORTH THE TRIP: GIRONA, SITGES & MONTSERRAT

If you want to taste life away from the big city, several easy and worthwhile one-day excursions suggest themselves.

Regular trains from Barcelona make a longish but rewarding day trip to **Girona** (91km, or 1½ hours, northeast) possible. Huddled in multicoloured confusion on the banks of the Onyar, this medieval town is delightful. The majestic **Catedral** (☎ 972 21 44 26; www.lacatedraldegirona.com; Plaça de la Catedral; museum admission €4, free on Sun; 🕑 10am-2pm & 4-7pm Tue-Sat Mar-Jun, 10am-8pm Tue-Sat Jul-Sep, 10am-2pm & 4-6pm Tue-Sat Oct-Feb, 10am-2pm Sun & holidays year-round), with its irregular Romanesque cloister and powerful Gothic interior, lords it over the rest of the town. Study Girona's history at the **Museu d'Història de la Ciutat** (☎ 972 22 22 29; Carrer de la Força 27; admission €2; 🕑 10am-2pm & 5-7pm Tue-Sat, 10am-2pm Sun) and wander the narrow streets of the medieval Jewish district around Carrer de la Força. Cross the river for the engaging **Museu del Cinema** (☎ 972 41 27 77; www.museudelcinema.org; Carrer de Sèquia 1; admission €3; 🕑 10am-8pm Tue-Sun May-Sep, to 6pm Tue-Fri, to 8pm Sat, 11am-3pm Sun Oct-Apr). You might just squeeze in a swift, early dinner, as the last train back down to Barcelona leaves around 9.20pm.

Only half an hour from Barcelona by train, **Sitges** is a unique resort that in summer attracts hordes of fashionable city folk and a huge international gay set. A former fishing village, it was a trendy hang-out for artists and bohemians in the 1890s and has remained one of Spain's more unconventional resorts ever since. It's no less attractive in winter, although you won't have much company as you cavort between its three **museums** (☎ 93 894 03 64; adult/child combined ticket €6.40/3.50; 🕑 10am-1.30pm & 3-6.30pm Tue-Fri, town hall back in the 1900s thought it would be amusing to have the three top Modernista architects line up for posterity. On just one block of the Passeig de Gràcia are three incredibly disparate houses, collectively known as the Manzana de la Discordia (Apple, or Block, of Discord): Gaudí's gaudy Casa Batlló (p103); Puig i Cadafalch's medieval-Dutch-looking Casa Amatller at No 41, whose foyer can be visited; and Domènech i Montaner's more rounded Casa Lleo Morera at No 35, which is visible only from the outside.

MUSEU DE CARROSSES FÚNEBRES

☎ 902 076902; www.funerariabarcelona.com; Carrer de Sancho d'Àvila 2, admission free; ⌚ 10am-1pm & 4-6pm Mon-Fri, 10am-1pm Sat, Sun & holidays; Ⓜ Marina
A somewhat morbid air pervades this collection of horse-drawn

10am-7pm Sat, to 3pm Sun Oct-Jun, 10am-2pm & 5-9pm Tue-Sun Jul-Sep), admire the sun-bleached baroque church atop a bluff over the beach, soak up the village atmosphere and wonder if it's too cold for a dip at the nude beach southwest of town.

Montserrat (Serrated Mountain) is the spiritual heart of Catalonia and your best opportunity to enjoy awesome scenery on a day trip from Barcelona. Comprising a massif of limestone pinnacles rising precipitously over gorges, this wondrous place has drawn hermits (er, independent travellers) since the 5th century. Perched up here is a **monastery** (☎ 93 877 77 01; www.abadiamontserrat.net; ⌚ 9am-6pm) and 12th-century chapel built to house **La Moreneta** (Black Virgin; ⌚ 8-10.30am & 12.15-6.30pm Mon-Sat, 8-10.30am, 12.15-6.30pm & 7.30-8.15pm Sun & holidays), a statue found nearby and venerated by hundreds of thousands of people each year. The **Museu de Montserrat** (Plaça de Santa Maria; admission €5.50; ⌚ 10am-6pm) has a varied art collection ranging from an Egyptian mummy to works by Degas and Caravaggio. Use the funiculars and walking paths to explore this incredible piece of nature.

For train timetables and prices from Barcelona to Girona and Sitges, check www.renfe.es. For Montserrat, the R5 line trains operated by FGC (www.fgc.es) run from Plaça d'Espanya station to Monistrol de Montserrat. They connect with the **cremallera** (rack-and-pinion train; www.cremallerademontserrat.com). One-way/return from Barcelona to Montserrat with the FGC train and *cremallera* costs €8/14.40. TransMontserrat tickets (€18.40) include the train, *cremallera*, two Metro rides, unlimited use of the funiculars in Montserrat and an audiovisual display on monastery life. For €31 you can have all this with the TotMontserrat card, which also includes museum entrance and a modest dinner at the self-service restaurant.

hearses (and a few motorised ones) used in the city from the 18th century until the 1950s. Some are decked out with life-size model horses and mannequins of funeral-company folk in full VIP gear of yesteryear.

MUSEU DEL PERFUM

93 216 01 46; www.museodel perfume.com; Passeig de Gràcia 39; adult/student & senior €5/3; 10.30am-2pm & 4.30-8pm Mon-Fri, 11am-2pm Sat; M Passeig de Gràcia;

Out back in the Regia perfume shop, this museum features hundreds of perfume receptacles and bottles, dating from predynastic Egypt to modern times, which you can look at but unfortunately not sniff.

MUSEU EGIPCI

93 488 01 88; www.fundclos.com; Carrer de València 284; adult/child €6/5; 10am-8pm Mon-Sat, to 2pm Sun; M Passeig de Gràcia;

This oddball private collection features more than 700 exhibits, including ceramics, mummies, friezes, jewellery, masks and statuettes from ancient Egypt.

PALAU DEL BARÓ QUADRAS

93 238 73 37; www.casaasia.es; Avinguda Diagonal 373; 10am-8pm Mon-Sat, to 2pm Sun; M Diagonal

Remodelled by Puig i Cadafalch between 1902 and 1904, this palace currently houses the Casa Asia cultural centre. It has fine stained glass and its façade is ornamented with detailed neo-Gothic carvings. Pop in for a cuppa at the café.

SHOP

ADOLFO DOMÍNGUEZ

Fashion

93 487 41 70; www.adolfodominguez .es; Passeig de Gràcia 32; 10am-8.30pm Mon-Sat; M Passeig de Gràcia

This Galician is one of Spain's most celebrated fashion designers. His

SHOPPING & SNACKING ON LA RAMBLA DE CATALUNYA

The city tourist board touts the shopping wonders of Passeig de Gràcia, but a wander along La Rambla de Catalunya (C4) is another experience, especially during the warmer months when a whole contingent of bars and restaurants put tables out on the broad, tree-lined pedestrian strip. Pop in and out of Furla (bags), Turkestan (rugs), Farrutx (shoes) Aramis (classic fashion) and a whole lot more. Don't miss the pastries in Mauri (p120). Stop for a coffee, beer or meal on the way and contemplate the décor of the many magnificent façades.

designs are classic and a little conservative, but it is timeless fashion for men and women, with exquisite tailoring and quality materials.

ALTAÏR *Books*

☎ 93 342 71 71; www.altair.es; Gran Via de les Corts Catalanes 616; 10am-2pm & 4.30-8.30pm Mon-Sat; M Universitat
If you need any encouragement in planning your next trip, these travel specialists will give you a nudge in the right direction. The range of local-interest books, guides to everywhere and maps is impressive.

ANTONIO MIRÓ *Fashion*

☎ 93 487 06 70; www.antoniomiro.es; Carrer del Consell de Cent 349; 10am-8.30pm Mon-Sat; M Passeig de Gràcia
The doyen of Barcelona couture, Antonio Miró made his name by producing elegant and unpretentious classic fashion of the highest quality for men and women. Miro also does an attractive line in accessories.

ARMAND BASI *Fashion*

☎ 93 215 14 21; www.armandbasi.com; Passeig de Gràcia 49; 10am-9pm Mon-Sat; M Passeig de Gràcia
Once the outfitter of James Bond and now doing design, Armand Basi is a stylish stalwart who does slinky numbers for the gals, uptown suits in black, evening wear and accessories.

BAD HABITS *Fashion*

☎ 93 487 22 59; Carrer de València 261; 10am-2pm & 4-8pm Mon-Fri; M Passeig de Gràcia
Bowl up to this bunker full of ballsy and original fashion for women unfazed by risk. Blurring the lines between feminine and masculine, colour and monochrome, Bad Habits stocks international labels as well as its own line.

BULEVARD DELS ANTIQUARIS *Antiques*

☎ 93 215 44 99; www.bulevarddelsantiquaris.com; Passeig de Gràcia 55 10am-8pm Mon-Sat; M Passeig de Gràcia
Part of the Bulevard Rosa shopping mall, this stretch is crammed with more than 70 antique shops tempting you with the this-and-thats of times gone by. A few of the specialist shops to look out for include Bruhuer (jewellery), Guvary's (porcelain dolls) and Victory (crystal).

BULEVARD ROSA *Shopping Arcade*

☎ 93 215 83 31; www.bulevardrosa.com; Passeig de Gràcia 55-57; 10.30am-8.30pm Mon-Sat; M Passeig de Gràcia
With more than 100 shops featuring some of the most interesting local designers of fashion and jewellery, this 1980s creation is the best mall in the city for style and a few hours of boutique-browsing.

CAMPER *Shoes*

☎ 93 215 63 90; www.camper.com; Carrer de València 249; ⌚ 10am-9pm Mon-Sat; Ⓜ Passeig de Gràcia

This classic Mallorcan shoe merchant continues to stamp all over the international market by successfully treading the fine line between rebellion and commercialism. There are branches all over town.

CASA DEL LLIBRE *Books*

☎ 93 272 34 80; www.casadellibro.com; Passeig de Gràcia 62; ⌚ 9.30am-9.30pm Mon-Sat; Ⓜ Passeig de Gràcia

This chain of general bookstores is among the best stocked in town. The 'home of the book' covers a broad range of subjects and has decent sections devoted to literature in English, French and other languages. It also organises readings and book presentations.

TAKE A SPIN ON THE SHOPPING BUS

The T1 Tombbús (aka Barcelona Shopping Line) route was set up for shoppers and runs from Plaça de Catalunya (E5) up Passeig de Gràcia then west on Avinguda Diagonal, taking in department stores and mainstream shopping precincts. It operates 8am to 9.30pm Monday to Saturday and costs €1.40. (The name means 'circle bus' and isn't necessarily an invitation to retail yourself into an early grave.)

EL CORTE INGLÉS *Department Store*

☎ 93 306 38 00; www.elcorteingles.es; Plaça de Catalunya 14; ⌚ 10am-10pm Mon-Sat; Ⓜ Catalunya

This monster of retail has everything you could possibly want and lots more that won't have crossed your mind. There's also a rooftop café with a splendid view. There are branches at Avinguda Diagonal 471 (A4), Avinguda Diagonal 617 (Map p133, C4) and Avinguda del Portal de l'Àngel 19 (Map pp76–7, A3).

ELS ENCANTS VELLS *Market*

☎ 93 246 30 30; Carrer del Dos de Maig (cnr Plaça de les Glòries Catalanes); ⌚ 7am-6.45pm Mon, Wed, Fri & Sat; Ⓜ Glòries

Barcelona's most authentic flea market is 'The Old Charms', where bargain-hunters riffle through everything from battered old shoes and bric-a-brac to antique furniture and new clothes. A lot of it is junk, but it depends on what's fallen off the back of the trucks the day you turn up. Go in the morning for the best choice.

FARRUTX *Shoes*

☎ 93 215 06 85; www.farrutx.com; Carrer de Rosselló 218; ⌚ 10am-2pm & 4.30-8.30pm Mon-Sat; Ⓜ Diagonal

Mallorca's Farrutx is one of the country's top shoemakers. It has been expertly dressing the heels of Barcelona's uptown women for decades, does a nice line in luxury sport shoes and tops it off with bags and other leather accessories.

FAVORITA *Design*

☎ 93 476 57 21; www.mueblesfavorita.com; Carrer de Mallorca 291; 10am-2pm & 4.30-8.30pm Mon-Sat; M Diagonal

You might not want to take furniture items back on the plane, but this contemporary design shop is worth a browse and a stop if only for the setting, a magnificent Modernista building constructed by Domènech i Montaner in 1895.

FLORISTERÍA NAVARRO *Florist*

☎ 93 457 40 99; www.floresnavarro.com; Carrer de València 320; 24hr; M Girona

Just met the love of your life? At 4am? Never fear, say it with flowers. This barnlike florist shop has flowers and plants for every conceivable situation. And it never closes.

FNAC *Department Store*

☎ 93 344 18 00; www.fnac.es; Plaça de Catalunya 4; 10am-10pm Mon-Sat; M Catalunya

This highly popular megastore – which is part of the French-owned chain – specialises in CDs, tapes, videos, books and video games. There's a useful ticket desk on the ground floor, which has lists of upcoming events and sells tickets. The main branch is located in El Triangle mall.

JOAN MURRIÀ *Food & Drink*

☎ 93 215 57 89; Carrer de Roger de Llúria 85; 9am-2pm & 5-8.30pm Tue-Fri, 10am-2pm & 5-8.30pm Sat; M Passeig de Gràcia

Classic both inside and out, this superb traditional-style grocer-delicatessen has been run by the same family since the early 1900s and continues to showcase the culinary wonders of Catalonia, Spain and beyond. Inspect the eye-catching façade featuring original designs by celebrated Modernista painter Ramón Casas.

JOAQUÍN BERAO *Jewellery*

☎ 93 215 00 91; www.joaquinberao.com; La Rambla de Catalunya 74; 10am-2pm & 5-8.30pm Mon-Sat; M Passeig de Gràcia

For something special, head to this elegant store showcasing the exquisite avant-garde creations of one of Spain's most prestigious jewellery designers. He works predominantly in silver and gold, and with new and entirely original concepts each season.

JOSEP FONT *Fashion*

☎ 93 487 21 10; www.josepfont.com; Carrer de Provença 304; 🕓 10am-8.30pm Mon-Sat; Ⓜ Diagonal

One of the leading women's fashion designers in Barcelona (with branches in Paris, Madrid and Bilbao), Font presents a line of daringly sleek and sexy items in no-nonsense colours. Peer inside for the minimalist décor alone.

LAIE *Books*

☎ 93 318 17 39; www.laie.es; Carrer de Pau Claris 85; 🕓 10am-9pm Mon-Sat; Ⓜ Urquinaona

A leisure complex for the mind, this bookshop combines a broad range of books with a splendid **café** (🕓 9am-9pm Mon, to 1am Tue-Sat), an international outlook and accommodating staff.

WINNING WAYS OF CATALAN WINES

Things have changed since Roman days, when wine from Catalonia was known throughout the empire as cheap and cheerful plonk. The Penedès region, about 40km southwest of Barcelona, is the biggest producer and best known for its bubbly, *cava* (Freixenet and Codorníu are household names around the world). Torres is the biggest label in still wines. Look out for wines with the El Priorat (strong, quality reds) and Raïmat (reds and whites) labels.

LOEWE *Accessories*

☎ 93 216 04 00; www.loewe.com; Passeig de Gràcia 35; 🕓 10am-8.30pm Mon-Sat; Ⓜ Passeig de Gràcia

International art critic Robert Hughes, in *Barcelona*, urges anyone with an interest in architecture not to patronise Loewe because of the vandalism it inflicted on this Domènech i Montaner Modernista building. If you're prepared to forgive the company – and it has tried to atone for its sin by undoing some of the changes it originally wrought to the façade – Loewe is one of the smartest international names in luxurious leather products.

MANGO *Fashion*

☎ 93 215 75 30; www.mango.es; Passeig de Gràcia 21; 🕓 10am-8pm Mon-Sat; Ⓜ Passeig de Gràcia

Begun in Barcelona in the 1980s, Mango has gone massive around the world with its combination of sexy and sassy couture, reliable fabrics and department-store prices. Slightly younger and funkier than its main rival, Zara (p118), Mango produces originals as well as pieces inspired by the big names.

MARC 3 *Gifts*

☎ 93 318 19 53; La Rambla de Catalunya 12; 🕓 10am-8.30pm Mon-Sat; Ⓜ Catalunya

Step inside this cavern of posters, prints and original paintings. At the

A FINE EIXAMPLE

Ildefons Cerdà conceived the grid-like Eixample (Extension) into which Barcelona grew from the late 19th century. However, developers disregarded its more utopian features, which called for building on only two sides of each block and the provision of gardens within. Now, nearly 150 years later, the city has reclaimed some of these public spaces. The garden (and toddlers' pool in summer) around the Torre de les Aigües water tower (E2) at Carrer de Roger de Llúria 56 offers an insight into what could have been. More such spaces (sans pool) are being opened up all the time.

front end of the shop is a remarkably wide range of items depicting the city you're in. A cut above the standard in kitsch, they can make fine gifts. Deeper inside is a host of other wall-decoration ideas, from Robert Doisneau to quality reproductions of classic ad posters.

MAS BACUS *Wine*

93 453 43 58; Carrer d'Enric Granados 68; 10am-10.30pm; FGC Provença

Bacus is the name and Bacchus is the game. This is one of several fine wine stores in this part of town. Staff can advise on your choice of local tipples and out the back there is a little gourmet tasting section with snacks to accompany the wine.

NORMA COMICS *Comics*

93 244 84 23; www.normacomics.com; Passeig de Sant Joan 7-9; 10.30am-2.30pm & 4.30-8.30pm Mon-Thu, 10.30am-8.30pm Fri & Sat; M Arc de Triomf

The largest comic store in the city (indeed the biggest comic-store chain in Europe) has a comic gallery, an astonishing international collection that stretches from *Batman* and *Tintin* through to Manga comics and more-or less porn items such as *Kiss*. Kids will love all the comic hero toys, too.

ROSER-FRANCESC *Fashion*

93 459 14 53; Carrer de València 285; 10.30am-2pm & 4.30-8.30pm Mon-Fri, 11am-2pm & 5-8.30pm Sat; M Passeig de Gràcia

Civilised and muted, the men's and women's collections in this store encompass a host of international labels along with local names such as Lydia Delgado, Antonio Miró and Konrad Muhr.

SEPHORA *Perfume*

93 306 39 00; www.sephora.es; El Triangle, Carrer de Pelai 13-17; 10am-10pm Mon-Sat; M Catalunya

This zebra-striped temple of fragrance is the largest in Europe and has every scent you've ever heard of, along with local flavours by the likes of Antonio Miró and Jesús del Pozo. A perfume organ allows you to experiment with your perfect eau, and if you don't come up smelling of roses, they'll happily exchange your fragrance.

VINÇON *Homeware*

☎ 93 215 60 50; www.vincon.com; Passeig de Gràcia 96; 10am-8.30pm Mon-Sat; M Diagonal

Despite its lofty reputation as the frame in which Spanish design evolves, this superb shop is relaxed and unpretentious. Pamper your aesthetic senses with a journey through its local and imported household wares. Wander upstairs and out onto the terrace for unusual sidelong views of La Pedrera (p109). The TincÇon (I'm Sleepy) annexe on Carrer de Rosselló 246 (C3) is in the same block and dedicated to the bedroom.

ZARA *Fashion*

☎ 93 318 76 75; www.zara.es; Passeig de Gràcia 16; 10am-9.30pm Mon-Sat; M Passeig de Gràcia

The Spanish name synonymous with inexpensive and good-quality smart casuals (that aren't made in sweatshops) will surely draw you in, if only because the same clobber in your home town probably costs twice as much! There are branches throughout the city.

Zara

EAT

ALBA GRANADOS

Mediterranean €€€

☎ **93 454 61 16; Carrer d'Enric Granados 34; ⏲ lunch & dinner Mon-Sat; FGC Provença;**

In summer, try for one of two romantic tables for two on the 1st floor balcony, truly unique in this town. Meat dishes are king here. The *carrillera de ternera* (a dark, soft meat from the neck of the cow) can be followed by exquisite desserts.

ALKÍMIA *Catalan* €€€

☎ **93 207 61 15; Carrer de l'Indústria 79; ⏲ lunch & dinner Mon-Fri, dinner Sat; M Sagrada Família**

Jordi Vila serves refined Catalan dishes with a twist in this white walled restaurant a few blocks from La Sagrada Família. Seafood dominates the menu in this one-star Michelin. Go for a set menu of about a dozen small courses – foodies' heaven.

AMALTEA *Vegetarian* €

☎ **93 454 86 13; Carrer de la Diputació 164; ⏲ lunch & dinner Mon-Sat ; M Urgell; V**

The weekday set lunch (€9) offers a series of dishes that change frequently with the seasons. Savour an *escalopa de seitan* (seitan escalope) and *empanadillas* (pastry pockets stuffed with spinach or hiziki algae and tofu).

CASA CALVET

Mediterranean €€€€

☎ **93 412 40 12; Carrer de Casp 48; ⏲ lunch & dinner Mon-Sat; M Urquinaona;**

Set on the ground floor of a Gaudí apartment block, this sophisticated restaurant is patronised by VIPs from far and wide, drawn by creative Mediterranean cooking with a Catalan bent. Savour Gaudí's genius as you enjoy your foie gras or ravioli stuffed with oysters.

CASA DARÍO *Seafood* €€€

☎ **93 453 31 35; Carrer del Consell de Cent 256; ⏲ lunch & dinner Mon-Sat, closed Aug; M Universitat**

This traditional Galician restaurant serves up a cornucopia of gifts of the sea. White jacketed waiters waft around with platters overflowing with scallops, octopus, crab and lobster, to name a few.

CATA 1.81 *Tapas* €€€

☎ **93 323 68 18; Carrer de València 181; ⏲ dinner Mon-Sat, closed August; M FGC Provença**

Treat yourself to a series of dainty gourmet dishes, such as *raviolis amb bacallà* (salt-cod dumplings) or *truita amb tòfona* (thick potato tortilla with a delicate trace of truffle). Since wines feature so prominently here, let rip with the list of fine Spanish tipples.

CERVESERIA CATALANA *Tapas* €€

☎ 93 216 03 68; Carrer de Mallorca 236; lunch & dinner; M Passeig de Gràcia;

Coffee and croissants are on in the morning, or wait until lunch to choose from the profusion of tapas and *montaditos (canapés)*. You can sit at the bar, on the footpath terrace or in the restaurant at the back. The variety of hot tapas, delectable salads and other snacks draws a well-dressed crowd (and we mean crowd) from all over the *barri*.

DOLSO *Dessert* €€

☎ 93 487 59 64; Carrer de València 227; lunch & dinner Mon-Sat, dinner Sun; M Passeig de Gràcia

There is an argument for skipping dessert wherever you lunch or dine and heading here instead (the only hitch is the 10.30pm closing time Sunday to Thursday). How about a *nemesí de chocolate* (a dense chocolate dessert fudge-cum-mousse smothered in passion fruit cream)? There are daily specials and some light savoury dishes. Round off with a cocktail (€7).

INOPIA *Gourmet Tapas* €€

☎ 93 424 52 31; Carrer de Tamarit 104; dinner Tue-Fri, lunch & dinner Sat; M Sant Antoni; V

Albert Adrià, brother of superchef Ferran, runs this bright, open, corner gourmet tapas bar to universal hurrahs. The featherweight tempura vegetables team up nicely with the chicken skewers. Getting a seat or spot at the bar can be a matter of patience.

MAURI *Café & Pastries* €

☎ 93 215 10 20; La Rambla de Catalunya 102; 8am-9pm Mon-Sat, to 3pm Sun; M Diagonal

Join the ladies who lunch for exquisite pastries, light snacks and piped music. The plush interior is capped by an ornately painted fresco at the entrance, which dates back to Mauri's first days in 1929. This is the kind of place that your mum would love.

PATAGONIA *Argentine* €€€

☎ 93 304 37 35; Gran Via de les Corts Catalanes 660; lunch & dinner Mon-Sat; M Passeig de Gràcia;

Argentine means beef in all its cuts and forms, and lots of it. You could ease your way in with empanadas, tiny pasty-type pies filled with, well, meat. Meat mains (you might want to skip the offal options) come with one of five side dishes.

SAÜC *Catalan* €€€€

☎ 93 321 01 89; Passagte de Lluís Pellicer 12; lunch & dinner Tue-Sat; M Hospital Clínic;

This basement spot is worth going the extra mile. Décor is neutral, allowing diners to concentrate on each mouthwatering course of creative Catalan cooking presented in the €56 tasting menu (appetiser, five courses, cheese selection and two desserts)!

SENSE PRESSA *Spanish* €€€

☎ 93 218 15 44; Carrer d'Enric Granados 96; lunch & dinner Tue-Sat, lunch Sun; M Diagonal

The name may mean 'not in a rush' but you'll need to hurry to book one of the six tables in this tiny treasury of Spanish cookery.

PUSHING THE BOAT OUT ON CARRER D'ARIBAU

From Thursday to Saturday nights the upper half of Carrer d'Aribau (B4) is transformed by the arrival of revellers from across town. Between Carrer de València and Avinguda Diagonal, the range of bars is astonishing. From white-jacket waiter cocktail bars to singalong dens, from Colombian dance spots to a Milan-style *aperitivo* joint, the place heaves. Later at night, a phalanx of bars, clubs and ill-disguised girlie bars bumps and grinds until dawn.

Some punters perch over gourmet tapas at the bar. Using only fresh market products, the menu ranges from *merluza al horno* (oven-baked hake) to a juicy *chuletón de buey* (huge T-bone steak).

SPEAKEASY *International* €€€€

☎ 93 217 50 80; Carrer d'Aribau 162-166; lunch & dinner Mon-Fri, dinner Sat; M Diagonal

Lurking behind the Dry Martini (p122) cocktail bar is this eatery with a 1930s feel. Head from the bar via the kitchen to an elegant 'storeroom' lined with hundreds of backlit bottles of quality tipples. The menu depends partly on the markets, but the carpaccio Dry Martini, a heavenly light meat treat, is a signature dish.

TAKTIKA BERRI *Basque & Tapas* €€€

☎ 93 453 47 59; Carrer de València 169; lunch & dinner Mon-Fri, lunch Sat; M Hospital Clínic

Deep in the grid maze of l'Eixample is this Basque redoubt. You have two choices: hang around the bar (just try at the lunch rush hour!) and nibble away at the army of Basque-style tapas – the trick is to grab them from the waitress as she transports them from the kitchen to the bar – or head out the back for a slap-up sit-down meal.

THAI GARDENS *Thai* €€€

93 487 98 98; Carrer de la Diputació 273; lunch & dinner Mon-Sat; M Passeig de Gràcia; V

One of the first and still one of the most authentic Thai experiences in town. The tall interior is filled with greenery and tables vary from intimate spots for two to big round affairs for festive groups. Take a nibble at a bit of everything with the set meal (€29).

DRINK

AIRE *Dance Bar*

93 487 83 42; www.arenadisco.com; Carrer de València 236; 11pm-3am Thu-Sat; M Passeig de Gràcia

Part of the Arena gay-disco chain, this is one of the most accessible lesbian dance bars in Barcelona. It's pretty relaxed and the gals can bring along their straight (male or female) friends for an evening of house and even pool.

BUDA BARCELONA *Bar & Restaurant*

93 318 42 52; www.budarestaurante.com; Carrer de Pau Claris 92; 9pm-3am Tue-Sun; M Urquinaona

The name bar and restaurant that is all the rage in Paris has its equally chic branch in the heart of L'Eixample. Come to eat, or pop in later for drinks at this luxurious Oriental den, and chill amid the beaming Buddhas. Tuesday night is Models Night, when doormen become rather tetchy.

DIETRICH GAY TEATRO CAFÉ *Cabaret*

93 451 77 07; Carrer del Consell de Cent 255; 10.30pm-3am; M Universitat

A classic of the Gaixample, this place hosts some of the best drag in the city in its elegant quarters – all timber finishings on two levels. Quiet during the week, it goes a little wild with drag shows, acrobats and dancing from Friday on.

DISTRITO DIAGONAL *Club*

Avinguda Diagonal 442; admission after 4am €15; 10pm-4am Wed & Thu, to 8am Fri & Sat; M Diagonal

It's long and narrow, with a wee, elevated dance floor at the back. What makes the place is the weekend opening hours. And before 4am, it's free. You can drink quietly enough at the bar or shake your thing until breakfast time.

DRY MARTINI *Cocktail Bar*

93 217 50 72; Carrer d'Aribau 162-166; 1pm-2am Sun-Thu, to 3am Fri & Sat; FGC Provença

For decades this has been one of the city's great cocktail joints, a classic of discreet, white-jacketed waiters who will whip up a fine, well, dry martini, or any other cocktail fantasy. Sit at the bar or plunge into the bloated, leather lounges. Out the back is the Speakeasy restaurant (p121).

HOTEL OMM BAR *Bar*

93 445 40 00; Carrer de Rosselló 265; 8am-midnight Sun-Thu, to 12.30am Fri & Sat; M Diagonal

Locals and guests mix in a sensual synergy in this uptown posers' bar that is highly agreeable if you feel like a little London–New York style attitude in a hip hotel setting. Just watching some of the less fiscally challenged cavort makes it worthwhile.

LES GENS QUE J'AIME *Bar*

93 215 68 79; Carrer de València 286; 6pm-2.30am; M Passeig de Gràcia

Incurably romantic, this basement bar in L'Eixample combines candle-light and privacy with antique red-velvet sofas and dark-wood furniture and trims. It's the perfect place for a night of sweet nothings.

MICHAEL COLLINS PUB *Pub*

93 459 19 64; Plaça de la Sagrada Família 4; noon-2.30am Sun-Thu, to 3am Fri & Sat; M Sagrada Família

Of all the many (and increasing number) of Irish pubs, this is one of the most agreeable. The Guinness is good and the punters, although many are foreigners, are generally residents rather than stag-night blow-ins.

SWEET CAFÉ *Bar*

http://sweetcafébcn.bogspot.com; Carrer de Casanova 75; 8pm-2.30pm Tue-Thu & Sun, to 3am Fri & Sat; M Urgell

This illuminated red tunnel of a bar is an eclectic drinking choice. Gay-friendly but by no means exclusive, it attracts a broad spectrum of punters, some in search of the occasional live band or events such as the Bollywood theme nights and art expos.

PLAY

ANTILLA BCN *Club*

93 451 45 64; www.antillasalsa.com; Carrer d'Aragó 141; 11pm-5am; M Urgell

The salsateca in town, this is the place to come for Cuban *son*, merengue, salsa and a whole lot more. If you don't know how to dance any of this, you may feel a little silly (as a bloke) but will probably get free lessons (if you're a lass). The blokes can come back at another time and pay for lessons.

ARENA MADRE *Club*

93 487 49 48; www.arenadisco.com; Carrer de Balmes 32; admission €5-10; 12.30-5am Mon-Sat, 7.30pm-5am Sun; M Universitat

Popular with a young gay crowd, Arena is one of the top clubs in town for boys seeking boys. Keep an eye out for striptease nights on Monday, drag shows on Wednesday and handbag nights on Thursday. There are three other Arena clubs nearby.

L'AUDITORI *Classical Music*

☎ 93 247 93 00; www.auditori.com; Carrer de Lepant 150; admission €10-45; box office noon-9pm Mon-Sat; M Monumental

The permanent home of Barcelona's symphony orchestra (OBC) is a starkly modern pleasure dome for serious music lovers, designed by renowned architect Rafael Moneo. Its comfortable (and acoustically unrivalled) main auditorium hosts orchestral performances, as well as occasional world-music jams. Chamber music is performed in a small, cosier and acoustically fabulous auditorium.

MASAJES A 1000 *Massage*

☎ 93 215 85 85; www.masajesa1000.com; Carrer de Mallorca 233; massages from €4; 7am-1am; FGC Provença

Sightseeing, eating, drinking and all that traffic noise can become a bit much. For a quick restorative massage, pop by here. A voucher system operates – the more vouchers you buy, the greater your options for longer and more specific massage treatment.

METRO *Club*

☎ 93 323 52 27; www.metrodiscobcn.com; Carrer de Sepúlveda 185; admission €10; midnight-5am Tue-Sun, 1am-5am Mon; M Universitat

Both dance floors here are absolutely heaving at weekends (and on weekday theme nights), when a 90% gay crowd thumps to top-of-the-range house and techno. During the week it's dance-club pop and handbags ahoy, with strip nights, bingo events and other animation, if you need any.

NEW CHAPS *Club*

☎ 93 215 53 65; Avinguda Diagonal 365; 9pm-3am Mon-Sat, 7pm-3am Sun; M Diagonal

As the name suggests, this bar is strictly for chaps – mostly mature, macho and suitably hirsute. It

GETTING LOOSE IN THE GAIXAMPLE

Gay bars and clubs are sprinkled across the city but especially concentrated in a small area of L'Eixample. Starting at the corner of Carrer de Balmes and Carrer del Consell de Cent (C5), move southwest along the latter, past the gay-oriented Hotel Axel (p172) and you will soon start running into bars, especially around Carrer de Muntaner (C5), Carrer de Casanova (C5) and Carrer de Villarroel (C6). If in doubt, just follow the crowds of beautiful boys cruising arm-in-arm on weekend evenings.

DEATH IN THE AFTERNOON

Although Catalans generally don't like bullfighting, the events have long been an integral part of the city's calendar. You can see them at 6pm on Sunday during the summer months at the **Plaça de Braus Monumental** (G2; ☎ 93 245 58 02; cnr Gran Via de les Corts Catalanes & Carrer de la Marina; Ⓜ Monumental). Tickets are available at the **arena** (🕐 11am-2pm & 4-8pm Mon-Sat, 10am-6pm Sun), through **ServiCaixa** (☎ 902 332211; www.servicaixa.com in Spanish) or at **Toros Taquilla Oficial** (C5; Carrer de Muntaner 26; Ⓜ Universitat).

attracts a regular jean- and leather-clad posse, and has theme nights and a shadowy downstairs with very dark room, labyrinth and sling.

RENOIR FLORIDABLANCA *Cinema*

☎ 93 426 33 37; www.cinesrenoir.com; Carrer de Floridablanca 135; admission €5.50-6.50; Ⓜ Urgell; ♿

This cinema, handy for the nearby El Raval area, is one of the city's better locations for movies, mainstream and off the wall, in the original language.

SALVATION *Club*

☎ 93 318 06 86; www.matineegroup.com; Ronda de Sant Pere 19-21; admission €10 🕐 midnight-5am Fri-Sun; Ⓜ Urquinaona

Salvation is the place for a big and beautiful gay night out. Two vast dance floors hammer out house and mainstream numbers and the gleaming torsos of the staff are part of the attraction – but strictly no touching.

TEATRE NACIONAL DE CATALUNYA *Theatre*

☎ 93 306 57 00; www.tnc.es; Plaça de les Arts 1; shows €8-32; 🕐 box office 3-8pm Tue-Sat & 1hr before show; Ⓜ Glòries/Monumental; ♿

This hi-tech, classical-looking temple to Catalan theatre was designed by Ricard Bofill. It offers a broad range of theatre (mostly in Catalan), contemporary dance and a mixed bag of international performances.

ZAC CLUB *Live Music*

☎ 93 321 09 22; www.zac-club.com; Avinguda Diagonal 477; admission €12-15; 🕐 10pm-5.30am; 🚌 6, 7, 33, 34, 63, 67 & 68

A top location for jazz, soul and blues fans, this uptown basement has undergone several name changes over time but remains true to its origins as one of the oldest live-music venues in Barcelona.

>GRÀCIA & PARK GÜELL

Gràcia was a separate village until 1897, when it was annexed to an expanding Barcelona. If only because of its tight, narrow lanes and endless interlocking squares, it has maintained a unique and separate identity.

Fashionable among bohemians in the 1960s and '70s, it is now being gentrified – people pay silly amounts for small flats here. There are few sights but the streets invite full immersion. The nooks and crannies, with everything from sushi bars to badly lit old taverns, are a source of endless fascination. North of the district lies one of Gaudí's extraordinary creations – the undulating Park Güell.

GRÀCIA & PARK GÜELL

SEE

Casa Museu Gaudí.........1 B1
Casa Vicenç.....................2 B4
Park Güell.......................3 B1

SHOP

Red Market.....................4 C4

EAT

Bilbao 5 D5
D.O 6 C4
Goliard...........................7 D5
Sol Soler 8 C4
Specchio Magico 9 C5

DRINK

Bar Canigó...................10 C4
Maria 11 C5
Raïm 12 D5

PLAY

Verdi 13 C4

A
B
C
D
Park Güell
VALLCARCA
EL CARMEL
0 200 m
0 0.1 miles
R del Guinardó
C de Larrard
C de Verdi
Av de l'Hospital Militar
C de l'Alegre de Dalt
C de l'Escorial
SANT GERVASI DE CASSOLES
Travessera de Dalt
C de Sant Salvador
C de Martí
Plaça de Lesseps
C de Pi i Margall
Lesseps
C de Torrent de l'Olla
C de Verdi
Plaça de la Virreina
GRÀCIA
C de Sant Lluís
Joanic
Plaça de la Torre
C de l'Or
C de la Perla
C de les Carolines
Plaça del Diamant
C de Topazi
C de Ramon y Cajal
Travessera de Gràcia
Fontana
C de Montseny
C dels Pons de Olano
Mercat de l'Abaceria Central
Av del Príncep d'Astúries
C de Balmes
Plaça del Sol
C del Planeta
C de Sant Pere Màrtir
Internet MSN
C de Torrent de l'Olla
C de la Llibertat
C de Lincoln
C Gran de Gràcia
Plaça de Rius i Taulet
C de Martínez de la Rosa
C de Progrés
C del Perill
Plaça de la Llibertat
C de Francisco Giner
Gràcia
FGC Plaça Molina
C de Mozart
Jardins de Moragas
C de Regàs
C de Vic
C de Maria de Jesús
C de Laforja
Via Augusta
C de la Riera de Sant Miquel
C de Bonavista
C de Còrsega
L'EIXAMPLE
C dels Madrazo
C de Maria Cubí
C de l'Avenir
C de Luis Antúnez
Plaça de Joan Carlos I
Av Diagonal
Travessera de Gràcia
C de Tuset
C de Seneca
C de Muntaner
C d'Aribau
C de Moià
Diagonal
Palau Robert Regional Tourist Office
C de Provença
Av Diagonal
C d'Enric Granados
C de Balmes
Diagonal
C de Rosselló
Pg de la Concepció
Pg de Gràcia
C de Londres
C d'Aribau
C de París
L'ESQUERRA DE L'EIXAMPLE

SEE

CASA MUSEU GAUDÍ

☎ 93 219 38 11; Park Güell, Carrer d'Olot 7; admission €4; 10am-8pm Apr-Sep, to 6pm Oct-Mar; M Lesseps/Vallcarca, 24

Worth a gander if you're in Park Güell (p21), this is the house where Gaudí spent many of his later years.

Roof mosaics, Park Güell

The museum includes furniture designed by Gaudí and his mates, along with personal effects and an ascetically narrow bed upon which he probably fantasised about completing La Sagrada Família.

CASA VICENÇ

Carrer de les Carolines 22; FGC Plaça Molina

The turreted and vaguely Mudéjar-inspired 1888 Casa Vicenç was one of Gaudí's first commissions. This private house (which cannot be visited) is awash with ceramic colour and shape.

PARK GÜELL

☎ 93 413 24 00; Carrer d'Olot 7; 10am-9pm Jun-Sep, to 8pm Apr, May & Oct, to 7pm Mar & Nov, to 6pm Dec-Feb; M Lesseps or Vallcarca, 24

Gaudí's fantasy public park was meant to be a glorious gated playground for Barcelona's rich, but that idea didn't come off (see p21). Instead, the town hall bought it in 1922 and opened it to the common folk. Just inside the main entrance on Carrer d'Olot, immediately recognisable by the two Hansel-and-Gretel gatehouses, visit the park's **Centre d'Interpretació** (☎ 93 285 68 99; adult/child under 16yr/student €2/free/1.50; 11am-3pm) in the Pavelló de Consergeria, the curvaceous, Gaudian former porter's home that

FORMULA FOR ADRENALINE

The motor-racing circuit at Montmeló, 20km northeast of the city, hosts the Spanish Grand Prix in late April or early May. Contact the **Circuit de Catalunya** (☎ 93 571 97 71; www.circuitcat.com; Carrer de Parets del Vallès, Montmeló) for details. Tickets cost €110 to €430. Purchase over the phone, at the track, online with **ServiCaixa** (☎ 902 332211; www.servicaixa.com in Spanish) or at advance-sales desks in El Corte Inglés department stores. You can get a regular *rodalies* (local) train to Montmeló (€1.30, 30 minutes) but will need to walk about 3km or find a local taxi (about €8 to €10) to reach the track. On race days the **Sagalés bus company** (☎ 902 130014) often puts on buses from Passeig de Sant Joan (Map pp104-5, E3), between Carrer de la Diputació and Carrer del Consell de Cent.

hosts a display on Gaudí's building methods and park history.

SHOP

RED MARKET *Fashion*

☎ 93 218 63 33; Carrer de Verdi 20; 5-9.30pm Mon, 11.30am-2pm & 5-9.30pm Tue-Sat; M Fontana

Carrer de Verdi is one of the most enticing streets in Gràcia. Home to everyone's favourite art-house cinema, a colourful series of eclectic bars and restaurants, and practical things like internet centres, it also hosts numerous little fashion boutiques. This shop is great for casual urban wear and accessories.

EAT

BILBAO *Spanish* €€€

☎ 93 458 96 24; Carrer del Perill 33; lunch & dinner Mon-Sat; M Diagonal

You'll need to book for generous portions of hearty Spanish grub (the emphasis is on juicy meat). The low-lit lamps, dusty bottles along the rear wall and attentive service will make you want to linger in what seems, from the outside, no more than a scruffy, neighbourhood bar.

D.O *Tapas* €€

☎ 93 218 96 73; Carrer de Verdi 36; dinner Mon-Fri, lunch & dinner Sat; M Fontana; V

A bright, perhaps overly lit spot, D.O serves *vins i platillos* (wine and little dishes). The accent is placed on the opportunity to taste various wines by the glass, accompanied by small dishes of anything from salads to seafood.

GOLIARD *Modern* €€

☎ 93 207 31 75; Carrer de Progrés 6; lunch & dinner Mon-Fri, dinner Sat & Sun; M Diagonal; V

This quiet diner is a haven of exquisite designer cooking at reasonable prices. Be sure to sample the *lassanya de pops i patates* (lasagne in which sliced potatoes take the place of pasta, and slightly spicy, tender octopus is the meat).

SOL SOLER *Tapas* €

☎ 93 217 44 40; Plaça del Sol 21-22; 5pm-1.30am Mon, 3pm-2am Tue-Fri, 1pm-2.30am Sat, 1pm-2am Sun; M Fontana; V

On a corner of the Gràcia district's liveliest *plaça,* this busy whole-

HANGING OUT IN GRÀCIA

Gràcia bubbles with life. Check out the Modernista market at Plaça de la Llibertat (B5) and the more down-to-earth produce market to the east, the Mercat de l'Abaceria Central (D4). Take a look at Gaudí's Casa Vicenç (p128) and then just wander. Swirl around with the locals in the bars and eateries, many of them gathered around a network of squares – the busiest are Plaça del Sol (C4) and Plaça de la Virreina (C3).

Plaça del Sol, Gràcia

food tapas bar has faded bohemian chic, relaxed music, intimate lighting and marble tables on which to enjoy a range of tasty fare – anything from couscous or lasagne to deep-fried chicken wings.

SPECCHIO MAGICO
Italian €€€

93 415 33 71; Carrer de Luis Antúnez 3; lunch & dinner; M Diagonal

Calm and charming, this tiny Italian joint is perfect for intimate get-togethers and is one of the most reliable Italian options in Barcelona. The pasta is truly *al dente,* with several varieties from the Puglia region (and the chance to taste a reasonable-quality *burrata* (a fresh Italian cheese made from buffalo mozzarella and cream).

 DRINK

BAR CANIGÒ *Bar*

93 213 30 49; Carrer de Verdi 2; 5pm-2am Mon-Thu, to 3am Fri & Sat; M Fontana

Especially welcoming in winter, this corner bar on an animated square is a timeless spot to simply sip on an Estrella beer around rickety old marble-top tables and indulge in animated banter. There's also a pool table.

MARIA *Bar*

Carrer de Maria 5; 9pm-3am; M Diagonal

For a great rock 'n' roll atmosphere, step back in time to this Gràcia classic. Play pool at the back or elbow your way to the bar for a beer or cocktail. Musical nostalgia takes care of the rest in this cramped but agreeable little bar.

RAÏM *Tavern*

Carrer de Progrés 34; 1pm-2am; M Diagonal

If you like your taverns unchanged since God knows when, with huge old wine barrels and a motley crew of punters from local guzzlers through to grunge Erasmus folk, this place could be for you. Judging by the wall-to-wall photos of Cuba, the owners have quite an affection for the island.

 PLAY

VERDI *Cinema*

93 238 79 90; Carrer de Verdi 32; admission €5.50-6.50; M Fontana;

This cinematic institution is highly regarded for championing creations left of centre and was the first to specialise in original-language movies. The location, surrounded by bars and restaurants, is an added incentive. It also runs Verdi Park, making nine screens between the two sites, in the next street over (Carrer de Torrijos 49).

>ZONA ALTA

The 'High Zone' is where most Barcelona folks with healthy bank accounts aspire to live, if possible in gated complexes or mansions with gardens (a rare luxury in Barcelona). To locals, the area really only refers to the hilly parts of town and Pedralbes, but for ease of orientation we have pushed the border down to Avinguda Diagonal (where you can ferret out some interesting nightlife and eating options) and let it overflow into Les Corts district (to include the all-important FC Barcelona club's Camp Nou stadium)!

Apart from expensive residential living, high points include Tibidabo, the Parc de Collserola, the CosmoCaixa science museum and monuments of Pedralbes.

ZONA ALTA

SEE

Name	No.	Grid
Bellesguard	1	B2
CosmoCaixa	2	C2
Museu de Ceràmica	3	B4
Museu de les Arts Decoratives	4	B4
Museu del Futbol Club de Barcelona	5	B5
Parc d'Atraccions	6	B1
Parc de Collserola	7	A1
Torre de Collserola	8	B1

SHOP

Name	No.	Grid
L'Illa del Diagonal	9	C4

EAT

Name	No.	Grid
Via Veneto	10	C4

DRINK

Name	No.	Grid
Berlin	11	D4
La Botellita	12	D4

PLAY

Name	No.	Grid
Bikini	13	C4
Búcaro	14	D4
Danzatoria	15	C2
Elephant	16	B4
Luz de Gas	17	D4
Mirablau	18	C2
Otto Zutz	19	D3
Sutton Club	20	D4

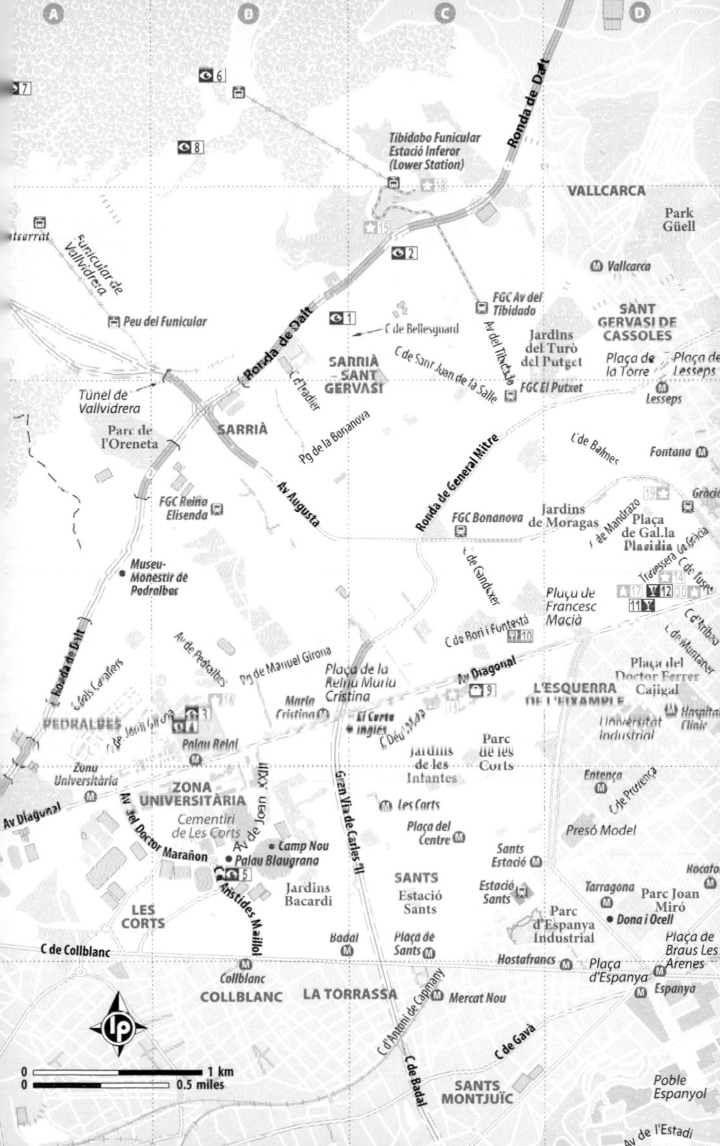
A
B
C
D
Ronda de Dalt
Tibidabo Funicular Estació Inferor (Lower Station)
VALLCARCA
Park Güell
Funicular de Vallvidrera
Peu del Funicular
Vallcarca
FGC Av del Tibidado
SANT GERVASI DE CASSOLES
C de Bellesguard
Jardins del Turò del Putget
Plaça de la Torre
Plaça de Lesseps
SARRIÀ - SANT GERVASI
C de Sant Joan de la Salle
Av del Tibidabo
FGC El Putxet
Lesseps
Túnel de Vallvidrera
SARRIÀ
Parc de l'Oreneta
Pg de la Bonanova
Ronda de General Mitre
C de Balmes
Fontana
Av Augusta
FGC Reina Elisenda
FGC Bonanova
Jardins de Moragas
Plaça de Gal.la Placidia
Gràcia
Museu-Monestir de Pedralbes
Travessera de Gràcia
C de Tuset
Plaça de Francesc Macià
C d'Aribau
C de Muntaner
C de Bori i Fontestá
Av de Pedralbes
Pg de Manuel Girona
Plaça de la Reina Maria Cristina
Av Diagonal
Plaça del Doctor Ferrer Cajigal
L'ESQUERRA DE L'EIXAMPLE
Maria Cristina
El Corte Inglés
Hospital Clínic
Universitat Industrial
PEDRALBES
Palau Reial
C Déu i Mata
Jardins de les Infantes
Parc de les Corts
Zona Universitària
ZONA UNIVERSITÀRIA
Entença
C de Provença
Les Corts
Av de Joan XXIII
Gran Via de Carles III
Cementiri de Les Corts
Av del Doctor Marañon
Camp Nou
Palau Blaugrana
Plaça del Centre
Presó Model
Sants Estació
SANTS
Estació Sants
Rocafor
Tarragona
Parc Joan Miró
C d'Arístides Maillol
Jardins Bacardi
LES CORTS
Parc d'Espanya Industrial
Dona i Ocell
C de Collblanc
Badal
Plaça de Sants
Plaça de Braus Les Arenes
Hostafrancs
Plaça d'Espanya
Espanya
Collblanc
COLLBLANC
LA TORRASSA
Mercat Nou
C d'Antoni de Campany
C de Gavà
C de Badal
0 1 km
0 0.5 miles
SANTS MONTJUÏC
Poble Espanyol
Av de l'Estadi
lp

SEE

BELLESGUARD

Carrer de Bellesguard; FGC Avinguda del Tibidabo

In typical Gaudí fashion, exposed brick, wrought iron and a sense of fairy-tale playfulness combine to give this private mansion, built in 1909, an unreal feel. It's a bit of a hike from the centre, so you need to be a fan of obscure things off beaten tracks.

COSMOCAIXA

93 212 60 50; www.fundacio.lacaixa.es; Carrer de Teodor Roviralta 47-51; adult/student €3/2; 10am-8pm Tue-Sun; 60, FGC Avinguda del Tibidabo;

Kids (and many grown-ups) can't help twiddling the knobs and engaging in experiments in this bright, playful science museum housed in a Modernista building (completed in 1909). The single greatest highlight of the site is the re-creation over 1 sq km of a chunk of flooded Amazon rain forest (Bosc Inundat), complete with anacondas and tropical downpours. Elsewhere in the complex, everything from fossils to physics is touched on.

MUSEU DE CERÀMICA

93 280 50 24; www.museuceramica.bcn.es; Palau Reial de Pedralbes, Avinguda Diagonal 686; adult/student €3.50/2 (incl Museu de les Arts Decoratives & Museu Tèxtil i d'Indumentària), free 1st Sun of month; 10am-6pm Tue-Sat, to 3pm Sun & holidays; M Palau Reial;

Welcome to perhaps the most fragile exhibition in Barcelona: an exceptional collection of Spanish ceramics dating from medieval times right up to the present day. The items on show include pieces by Miró and Picasso, as well as a charming selection of tiles depicting Catalan life.

FOLLOW THE BALLS

Passions run high in Barcelona over the fate of its star league football side, Football Club Barcelona (p22). The team plays at the **Camp Nou stadium** (B5; 902 189900; www.fcbarcelona.com; Carrer d'Aristides Maillol, Les Corts; tickets €30-120; box office 9am-1.30pm & 3.30-6pm Mon-Fri; M Collblanc), and tickets for the big matches can be quite hard to come by. Touts always work the stadium, but you need to be careful, as security is tight. The same club boasts a champion basketball team. FC Barcelona shoots baskets at the Palau Blaugrana (B5), just by the main stadium. Tickets cost about €13 to €40.

WORTH THE TRIP: CONVENT LIFE AT THE MUSEU-MONESTIR DE PEDRALBES

This peaceful **museum** (A4; ☎ 93 203 92 82; www.museuhistoria.bcn.es; Baixada del Monestir 9; admission, incl Museu d'Història de la Ciutat & Park Güell Centre d'Interpretació, €4; 10am-5pm Tue-Sat, to 3pm Sun Jun-Sep, to 2pm Tue-Sat, to 3pm Sun Oct-May) provides an absorbing insight into medieval monastic life. The convent was founded in 1326 and is a jewel of Catalan Gothic with its three-storey cloister. The few remaining nuns have moved to nearby quarters. Around the cloister, visit the restored refectory, kitchen, stables, stores and infirmary. Built into the cloister walls are day cells where the nuns spent most of their time in prayer and devotional reading. To get there take the FGC train to Reina Elisenda or bus 22, 63, 64 or 75.

Tile detail, Monestir de Pedralbes

MUSEU DE LES ARTS DECORATIVES

93 280 50 24; www.museuartsdecoratives.bcn.es; Palau Reial de Pedralbes, Avinguda Diagonal 686; adult/student €3.50/2 (incl Museu de Ceràmica & Museu Tèxtil i d'Indumentària), free 1st Sun of month; 10am-6pm Tue-Sat, to 3pm Sun & holidays; M Palau Reial;

Occupying the same former palace as the Museu de Ceràmica, this series of galleries overlooks a stunningly sumptuous oval throne room and features a collection of furniture and decorative objects from the early Middle Ages to the kitsch 1970s.

MUSEU DEL FUTBOL CLUB DE BARCELONA

93 496 36 08; www.fcbarcelona.es; Carrer d'Aristides Maillol; adult/child €6/4.50; 10am-6.30pm Mon-Sat, to 2.30pm Sun & holidays; M Collblanc;

The museum dedicated to one of the Europe's greatest football clubs is a big draw. Among the quirkier paraphernalia are old sports board games, a 19th-century leather football, the life-size diorama of a dressing room in the days of yore, posters and magazines from way back and the *futbolín* (table soccer) collection. You can join a guided **tour** (adult/child €10.50/8; 10am-5.30pm Mon-Sat, to 1.30pm Sun & holidays) of the stadium.

PARC D'ATRACCIONS

93 211 79 42; www.tibidabo.es; Plaça de Tibidabo 6; rides & Museu d'Autòmats €11, access to all rides €22, children under 1.2m €9; noon-10pm or 11pm Wed-Sun Jul–early-Sep, other closing times vary (from 5pm to 9pm) Sat, Sun, holidays & other days in warmer months; FGC Avinguda del Tibidabo, then Tramvia Blau & funicular

For the Ferris-wheel ride of your life – with the bonus of panoramic views from the top of Tibidabo – head for this cherished old-fashioned fun fair (p32). It has all the usual thrills as well as the remarkable Museu d'Autòmats del Tibidabo, where you can see carnival games and gizmos from the 19th century. One of the scariest attractions is the Krueger Hotel. Enter this house of horrors and be prepared to have your nerves rattled by ghouls and crims leaping out at you from the darkness.

PARC DE COLLSEROLA

93 280 35 52; www.parccollserola.net; Carretera de l'Església 92; Centre d'Informació 9.30am-3pm; FGC Baixador de Vallvidrera

Some 8000 hectares of parkland spread out in the hilly country southwest of Tibidabo, forming a marvellous escape hatch for city folk needing a little nearby nature. Pick up information at the Centre d'Informació.

TORRE DE COLLSEROLA

93 406 93 54; www.torredecollserola.com; Carretera de Vallvidrera; adult/child €5.20/3.60 11am-2.30pm & 3.30-7pm Wed-Sun; FGC Avinguda del Tibidabo, then Tramvia Blau & funicular;

Designed by Britain's Sir Norman Foster, this 288m telecommunications tower was built to bring the events of the 1992 Olympics to TV viewers around the world. A glass lift shoots up to an observation deck at 115m that affords splendid views of Tibidabo and the city.

Torre de Collserola

Joan Miró's *Dona i Ocell*

MONUMENTAL MIRÓ

One of the symbols of Barcelona, *Dona i Ocell* (D5; Woman and Bird) was Joan Miró's last substantial sculpture. It was inaugurated in 1981, the year of his death, in what is now known as Parc Joan Miró.

SHOP

L'ILLA DEL DIAGONAL

Department Store

☎ 93 444 00 00; www.lilla.com; Avinguda Diagonal 545; 10am-9.30pm Mon-Sat; M Maria Cristina

This shopping centre, situated in the heart of the business district caters to uptowners and houses swanky designer stores and all the usual chains. In its heyday it was acclaimed for its architectural style.

EAT

VIA VENETO *Catalan* €€€€

☎ 93 200 72 44; Carrer de Ganduxer 10; lunch & dinner Mon-Fri, dinner Sat; FGC La Bonanova

Some places are just evergreens. This high–so-ciety restaurant (and don't forget to dress up!) has maintained its excellent service and standards since it first opened its doors in 1967. The vaguely Art Deco setting sees the *crème de la crème* of the city sitting down to some exquisitely prepared dishes such as *llebre a la royal amb pomes saltades al Calvados* (hare with apples sautéed in Calvados, €42).

DRINK

BERLIN *Bar*

☎ 93 200 65 42; Carrer de Muntaner 240; 🕐 10am-1.30am Mon-Wed, to 3am Thu-Sat; M Diagonal/Hospital Clínic

This elegant corner bar with pavement tables also has designer lounges downstairs for sprawling while slurping. There is a relaxed feeling about the place, with a mixed group of punters. Relaxation stops at closing time, however, as these people want you out fast! Head for Luz de Gas (p141) next door to continue the fun of the evening.

LA BOTELLITA *Bar*

Carrer d'Aribau 191; admission Fri & Sat €8; 🕐 10pm-3.30am Thu-Sat; M Diagonal

This is a fiery uptown establishment that will really get your motor running before you start hitting the clubs. Head upstairs to a kind of narrow gangway. Once here you will understand why the place is called the Little Bottle. Behind the bar are little minibar-style bottles of all your preferred poisons, and that's what you are served.

PLAY

BIKINI *Live Music*

☎ 93 322 00 05; www.bikinibcn.com; Carrer Déu i Mata 105, Les Corts; admission €14 🕐 midnight-5am Wed-Sat; M Entença

The reincarnation of a legendary club that was torn down in 1990 to make way for a shopping mall, the modern Bikini is regarded by many as the best venue in Barcelona, with crisp acoustics and diverse programming. There are three main performance areas, and virtually all genres are catered for.

BÚCARO *Bar-Club*

☎ 93 209 65 62; Carrer d'Arlbau 195; admission Fri & Sat €10; 🕐 11pm-3.30am Sun-Wed, to 5am Thu-Sat; M Diagonal

The doormen are pretty relaxed at this bar-cum-club. The long lounge area where you enter is great for sipping and chilling, while out the back the music makes conversation redundant and close-in dancing inevitable. Upstairs is another quieter bar area.

DANZATORIA *Club*

☎ 93 211 62 61; www.danzatoria-barcelona.com; Avinguda del Tibidabo 61; €15 🕐 9pm-3am; FGC Tibidabo and/or taxi

Set in a 19th-century mansion amid gardens, this is one of the most sensual places to get your

Veronika Brinkmann,
Director of Group Sales, Hotel Arts Barcelona

What brought you to Barcelona? I have Spanish blood and always wanted to live in Spain, but I planned on Madrid. **What happened?** I ca to Barcelona for a weekend and within a few hours I knew I'd come to live here. **Where would you stay on a visit?** In the 34th floor penthous in Hotel Arts…if I could afford it, that is! **What's fun at night?** I love the clubs with outdoor space, like Elephant, or Danzatoria up on Tibidabo. **when the sun don't shine?** The foyer bar in Hotel Omm. It's very Londo **So you drink there but you wouldn't sleep there?** Ha ha! **Where do y head for a splash?** The local beaches have great ambience, with *chiringuitos* (beach bars) playing music into the night. My favourite beach is Bogatell – I'm looking to buy a house nearby!

dance night started. The chill out doubles as a restaurant (book) until midnight, and you can head through to a house hall, R&B section or lounge in hammocks with a flute of champagne in the gardens.

ELEPHANT *Club*

93 334 02 58; www.elephantbcn.com; Passeig dels Til.lers 1; admission Fri & Sat €15; 11pm-3am Wed, to 5am Thu-Sun M Palau Reial

If you can manage to turn up here in a convertible, so much the better. This is like being invited to a celebs' garden party. Inside the big tentlike dance space things can heat up musically as the night wears on, but plenty of people just hang in the gardens with their cocktails.

LUZ DE GAS *Live Music & Club*

93 209 77 11; www.luzdegas.com; Carrer de Muntaner 244-246; admission up to €20; 11.30pm-5am; M Diagonal

Anything goes at this large and happening music hall that hosts residencies and big international names of soul, country, salsa, rock, jazz, pop and cabaret in a beautiful *belle époque* setting. The versatile place converts into a thumping club with something of a meat-market reputation. Next door, in Sala B, the pace is slower and the bars plentiful over two floors.

MIRABLAU *Club*

93 418 58 79; Plaça del Doctor Andreu, Tibidabo; bar 11am-5am; FGC Tibidabo, then Tramvia Blau/taxi

For the most stunning views of Barcelona – and the spectacle of the city's rich and famous dancing badly – head for this chichi bar and club. Doormen come on for the club at 11pm, and it helps if you're wearing Prada to get past them.

OTTO ZUTZ *Club*

93 238 07 22; Carrer de Lincoln 15, Sant Gervasi; admission €15; midnight-5.30am Tue-Sat; FGC Gràcia

This converted three-storey warehouse remains one of the sexiest and snootiest dance dens in Barcelona. There's a different vibe on the three floors (top floor is VIPs only), which are linked by a giant atrium.

SUTTON CLUB *Club*

93 414 42 17; www.thesuttonclub.com; Carrer de Tuset 13; admission €12; 11.30pm-6am Thu-Sat; M Diagonal

An uptown honey pot, this place doesn't get happening until surrounding bars start closing their doors. It's a den of coke-snorting beautiful people, and the central dance area (complete with go-go girls and boys), surrounded arena-style by seating and several strategically placed bars, will draw you in.

>MONTJUÏC, SANTS & POBLE SEC

Overlooking the sea, Montjuïc hill is a cornucopia of activities. Locals escape here for a breath of fresh air. A series of pretty gardens could occupy much of a lazy day, but there is plenty to see, from the Castell de Montjuïc at the hill's apex to the Fundació de Joan Miró and majestic Museu Nacional d'Art de Catalunya. Nearby are more museums, the Olympic stadium, pools, concert venues and the Poble Espanyol, a composite of Spanish towns in miniature.

Several inviting eateries and bars line the higgledy-piggledy streets of Poble Sec, which slopes down the north face of the hill. And theatre-goers are spoiled for choice at the foot of the hill.

MONTJUÏC, SANTS & POBLE SEC

SEE

CaixaForum....1 D2
Fundació Joan Miró....2 E3
Galería Olímpica....3 E4
Jardí Botànic....4 E4
Jardins de Joan Brossa....5 F3
Jardins de Mossèn Cinto Verdaguer....6 F3
Jardins de Mossèn Costa i Llobera....7 G3
La Font Màgica....8 D2
L'Anella Olímpica & Estadi Olímpic....9 E4
Museu d'Arqueologia de Catalunya....10 E3
Museu Etnològic....11 E3
Museu Militar....12 F4
Museu Nacional d'Art de Catalunya (MNAC)..13 D3
Parc d'Espanya Industrial....14 B1
Pavelló Mies van der Rohe....15 D2
Poble Espanyol....16 C3

SHOP

Elephant....17 F2

EAT

Elche....18 G2
La Bella Napoli....19 F2
Quimet i Quimet....20 F2

DRINK

Maumau Underground.21 G2
Tinta Roja....22 F2

PLAY

Piscines Bernat Picornell....23 D3
Sala Apolo....24 G2
Tablao de Carmen....25 C3
Teatre Lliure....26 E2
Terrrazza....27 D3

Please see over for map

 SEE

CAIXAFORUM

☎ 93 476 86 00; www.fundacio.lacaixa.es; Avinguda del Marquès de Comillas 6-8; 10am-8pm Tue-Sun; M Espanya; Housed in a former Modernista factory, an outstanding brick caprice by Josep Puig i Cadafalch, this extensive private collection of contemporary art is in constant flux. The Caixa building society rotates its international line-up of works and organises frequent temporary exhibitions, which means that no two visits will be the same. Among the names in the permanent collection are such Spanish icons as Antoni Tàpies and Miquel Barceló.

FUNDACIÓ JOAN MIRÓ

☎ 93 443 94 70; www.bcn.fjmiro.es; Plaça de Neptu; adult/senior & child €7.50/5, temporary exhibitions extra €4/3; 10am-7pm Tue, Wed, Fri & Sat, to 9.30pm Thu, to 2.30pm Sun & holidays; 50, 55, 61 & PM; Joan Miró left his hometown this art foundation, a homage to himself, in 1971. Its light-filled buildings are crammed full with a broad spectrum of Miró's life work, from early sketches to giant, bold canvasses. The collection comprises around 300 paintings, 150 sculptures, some textiles and more than 7000 drawings spanning his entire life, although only a small portion is ever on display. 'A Joan Miró'

Rooftop installations, Barcelona's Fundació Joan Miró.

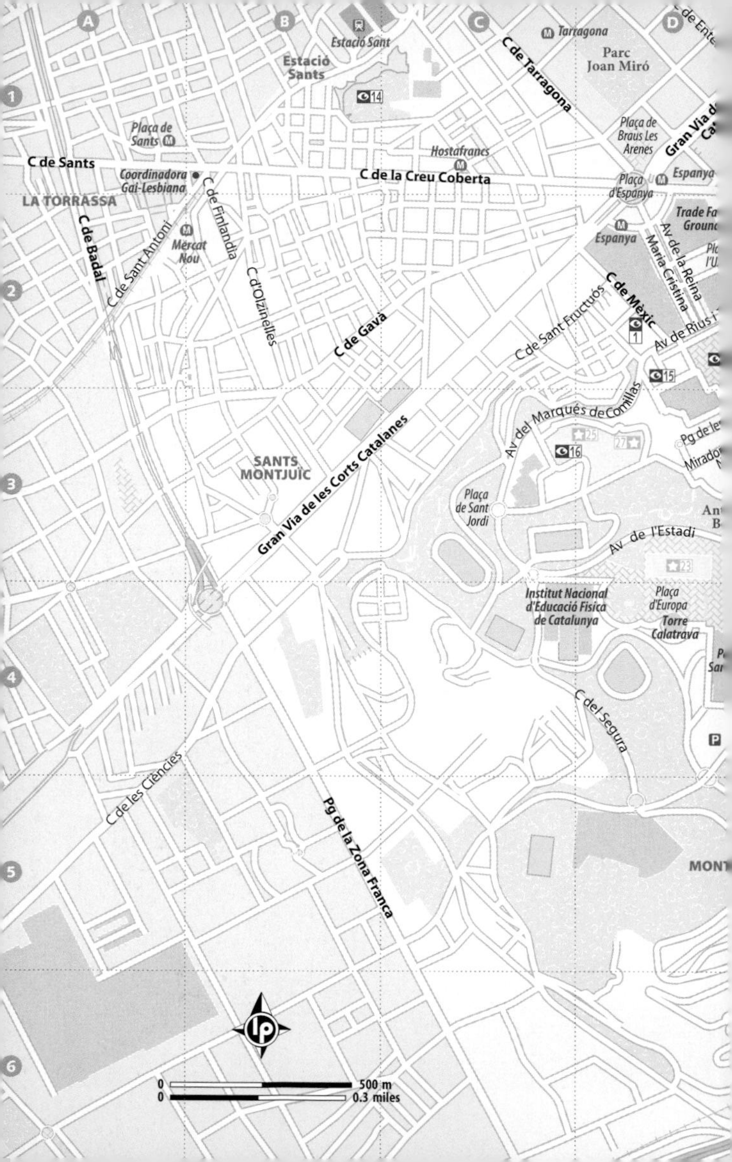
A
B
C
D
1
2
3
4
5
6
Estació Sant
Estació Sants
14
Tarragona
Parc Joan Miró
C de Tarragona
Plaça de Sants
Plaça de Braus Les Arenes
Gran Via de
C de Sants
Hostafrancs
Coordinadora Gai-Lesbiana
C de la Creu Coberta
Plaça d'Espanya
Espanya
LA TORRASSA
C de Finlandia
C de Badal
C de Sant Antoni
Mercat Nou
Trade Fa Groun
Espanya
Av de la Reina Maria Cristina
C d'Olzinelles
C de Mèxic
C de Sant Fructuós
1
C de Gavà
Av de Rius i
15
Av del Marquès de Comillas
25
27
Pg de le
Mirado
16
Gran Via de les Corts Catalanes
SANTS MONTJUÏC
Plaça de Sant Jordi
Av de l'Estadi
23
Institut Nacional d'Educació Física de Catalunya
Plaça d'Europa
Torre Calatrava
C del Segura
P
C de les Ciències
Pg de la Zona Franca
MONT
0
500 m
0
0.3 miles

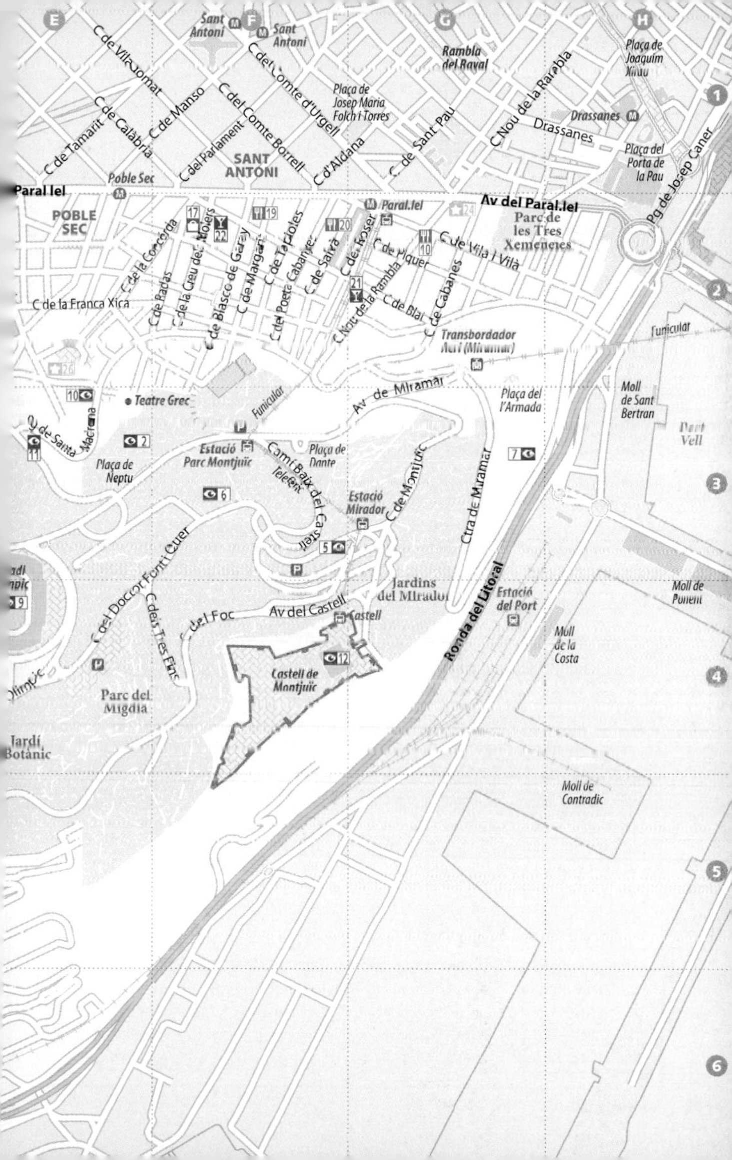

E
F
G
H
1
2
3
4
5
6
Sant Antoni
C de Viladomat
C del Comte d'Urgell
Plaça de Josep Maria Folch i Torres
Rambla del Raval
Plaça de Joaquim Xirau
C Nou de la Rambla
Drassanes
C de Tamarit
C de Calàbria
C de Manso
C del Parlament
C del Comte Borrell
SANT ANTONI
C d'Aldana
C de Sant Pau
Plaça del Porta de la Pau
Pg de Josep Caner
Poble Sec
Paral.lel
POBLE SEC
Av del Paral.lel
Parc de les Tres Xemeneies
C de la Concòrdia
C de Blasco de Garay
C de Margarit
C de Tapioles
C del Poeta Cabanyes
C de Salvà
C de Piquer
C de Vila i Vilà
C de Cabanes
C de Blai
C de la Franca Xica
C de Radas
C Nou de la Rambla
Transbordador Aeri (Miramar)
Funicular
Teatre Grec
Av de Miramar
Plaça del l'Armada
Moll de Sant Bertran
Port Vell
C de Santa Madrona
Estació Parc Montjuïc
Plaça de Dante
Camí Baix del Castell
Telefèric
Plaça de Neptu
Estació Mirador
C de Montjuïc
Ctra de Miramar
C del Doctor Font i Quer
Jardins del Mirador
Moll de Ponent
Av del Castell
Castell
C del Foc
C dels Tres Pins
Estació del Port
Ronda del Litoral
Moll de la Costa
Castell de Montjuïc
Parc del Migdia
Jardí Botànic
Moll de Contradic

is a collection of work by other contemporary artists, donated in tribute to Miró and held in a basement hall.

GALERÍA OLÍMPICA

☎ 93 426 06 60; www.fundaciobarcelonaolimpica.es; Passeig Olímpic s/n; adult/senior & child under 12yr/student €2.70/1.50/2.40; 10am-1pm & 4-6pm Mon-Fri; 50, 61 & PM;

This museum is chock-full of photographs and memorabilia associated with the 1992 Barcelona Olympics. Favourite items are the scrumptious-looking models of the standard daily diet (baked beans, anyone?) of cyclists and gymnasts.

JARDÍ BOTÀNIC

☎ 93 426 49 35; www.jardibotanic.bcn.es; Carrer del Doctor Font i Quer; adult/student €3/1.50, free last Sun of month; 10am-8pm Jul & Aug, to 5pm Mon-Fri, to 8pm Sat & Sun & holidays Apr-Jun & Sep, to 5pm Oct-Mar; 50, 61 & PM;

Concentrating on a 'Mediterranean' flora theme, this botanic garden features thousands of species that thrive in similar climates all over the world, from Spain to Turkey, Australia to South Africa and California to Chile.

JARDINS DE JOAN BROSSA

Carrer de Montjuïc; 10am-sunset;

These varied gardens and play areas spread out over what was once a funfair. For more about the gardens see p26.

JARDINS DE MOSSÈN CINTO DE VERDAGUER

Camí Baix del Castell; 10am-sunset;

These beautiful, cool gardens are devoted to bulbs and aquatic plants, from tulips to water lilies. See also p26.

JARDINS DE MOSSÈN COSTA I LLOBERA

Montjuïc; 10am-sunset;

A longish wander downhill from the Castell de Montjuïc, these gardens are of particular interest for the collection of tropical and desert plants – including a veritable forest of cacti. See also p26.

WHO'S THE KING OF THE CASTLE?

In 2005, Spain's Socialist prime minister, José Luis Rodríguez Zapatero, promised to hand Castell de Montjuïc (Montjuïc castle; F4) from the military to the city of Barcelona, which wants to turn this symbol of repression into a 'peace museum'. So far the Ministry of Defence has stalled, insisting that the Spanish flag continue to fly here after any such handover, something Barcelona is not so keen on.

LA FONT MÀGICA

Avinguda de la Reina Maria Cristina; every half hour 7-8.30pm Fri & Sat Oct-late Jun, 9.30-11.30pm Thu-Sun late Jun-Sep; M Espanya;

Delightfully over the top, the biggest of Montjuïc's famous fountains splashes into life with an irresistible summer-evening extravaganza of music and light. Whether it's to the tune of Tchaikovsky or Abba, you'll be mesmerised by the waterworks.

L'ANELLA OLÍMPICA & ESTADI OLÍMPIC

Avinguda de l'Estadi; 10am-6pm Oct-Apr, to 8pm May-Sep; M Paral.lel, then Funicular de Montjuïc, or 50, 61 & PM

One for sports fans. L'Anella Olímpica (Olympic Ring) is the group of installations built for the main events of the 1992 Olympics. They include the Estadi Olímpic, which is open to the public when Espanyol (the 'other' football team) isn't getting whipped.

L'Anella Olímpica

MUSEU D'ARQUEOLOGIA DE CATALUNYA

☎ 93 424 65 77; www.mac.es; Passeig de Santa Madrona 39-41; adult/child €2.40/1.70; 9.30am-7pm Tue-Sat, 10am-2.30pm Sun; 55 & PM;

This archaeology museum mainly features artefacts discovered in Catalonia and Mediterranean Spain, ranging from copies of pre-Neanderthal skulls to jewel-studded Visigothic crosses. It also houses a statue of a splendidly endowed, and routinely aroused, Priapus (the god of male procreative power) that we're not allowed to inspect closely.

MUSEU ETNOLÒGIC

☎ 93 424 64 02; www.museuetnologic.bcn.es; Passeig de Santa Madrona 16-22; adult/child under 12yr/senior & student €3/free/1.50, free 1st Sun of month; noon-8pm Tue-Sat, 11am-3pm Sun late Jun-late Sep, 10am-7pm Tue & Thu, 10am-2pm Wed, Fri & Sun late Sep-late Jun; 55;

Ètnic, the permanent exhibition, includes several thousand wide-ranging items on show in three themed sections: Orígens (Origins), Pobles (Peoples) and Mosaics. Along with lots of material from rural areas of Catalonia and parts of Spain, the museum's collections include items from as far afield as Australia, Japan and Morocco.

MUSEU MILITAR

☎ 93 329 86 13; Castell de Montjuïc; admission €2.50; 9.30am-5pm Tue-Sun Nov–mid-Mar, to 8pm Tue-Sun mid-Mar–Oct; PM;

An assortment of weapons, uniforms, armour, tin soldiers and instruments of war from down the centuries make up this sombre collection, housed in an 18th-century fortress (more often used for bombarding the city than defending it) that overlooks Barcelona. The view from the ramparts is magnificent.

MUSEU NACIONAL D'ART DE CATALUNYA (MNAC)

☎ 93 622 03 76; www.mnac.es; Mirador del Palau Nacional; adult/senior & child under 12yr/student €8.50/free/6; 10am-7pm Tue-Sat, to 2.30pm Sun & holidays; M Espanya;

The grandest and worthiest of all Barcelona's art museums, the MNAC gathers under one roof a plethora of Catalan works that range from the Middle Ages to well into the 1900s. The Romanesque art in particular is a unique experience (see p14).

PARC D'ESPANYA INDUSTRIAL

Carrer de Sant Antoni, Sants; 10am-sunset; M Sants Estació;

Maligned by many, this playfully postmodern park comprises what look like galactic watchtowers overlooking a boating lake and a dragon sculpture that's popular with kiddies. It's transformed when illuminated at night and worth a look if you're waiting for a train at Estació Sants.

PAVELLÓ MIES VAN DER ROHE

93 423 40 16; www.miesbcn.com; Avinguda del Marquès de Comillas; adult/child under 18yr/student €3/free/2; 10am-8pm; M Espanya;

This is a replica of a structure erected for – and demolished with – the 1929 World Exhibition. In hindsight it was considered a milestone of modern architecture and was rebuilt in 1986. With a light and airy design comprising horizontal planes, it reveals Mies van der Rohe's vision of a new urban environment.

POBLE ESPANYOL

93 508 63 30; www.poble-espanyol.com; Avinguda del Marquès de Comillas; adult/child under 12yr/concession €7.50/4/5.50; 9am-8pm Mon, to 2am Tue-Thu, to 4am Fri & Sat, to midnight Sun; M Espanya;

Something of an imposter, the Spanish Village was put together for the 1929 World Exhibition. It comprises replicas of famous buildings and examples of traditional architecture from all over Spain. For a tourist trap, it's quite engaging, but its craft shops, restaurants and bars share the unfortunate distinction of being overpriced.

SHOP

ELEPHANT *Books*

93 443 05 94; Carrer de la Creu dels Molers 12; 10am-8pm Mon-Sat; M Poble Sec

This bright bookshop is off the main tourist tracks but is a helpful haven of books in the Queen's English. Stock ranges from fiction to kids' stuff, with a smattering of reference works and a healthy secondhand section.

EAT

ELCHE *Catalan* €€

93 441 30 89; Carrer de Vila i Vilà 71; lunch & dinner; M Paral.lel;

Some places are just good at what they do, and keep doing it. Hidden away from the busy old-town centre, this old-style restaurant over two floors has been serving up a variety of paellas, rice dishes and *fideuá* (similar to paella, but made with vermicelli noodles) since the 1960s. To enliven the atmosphere, order a bottle or two of *turbio*, a simple, cloudy white wine.

LA BELLA NAPOLI *Italian* €€

☎ 93 442 50 56; Carrer de Margarit 12; lunch Tue, lunch & dinner Wed-Sun; M Paral.lel;

Never will the Catalans seem so much the dour lot they are sometimes made out to be as when you descend into this isle of Neapolitan nuttiness. The staff are mostly from Naples or thereabouts, full of teasing humour and bring you some of the best pizza in Barcelona.

QUIMET I QUIMET *Tapas* €€

☎ 93 442 31 42; Carrer del Poeta Cabanyes 25; lunch & dinner Tue-Sat, lunch Sun; M Paral.lel;

This postage stamp–sized tapas bar is a gourmet paradise in miniature. Let the bar staff combine a few canapés, seafood tapas, cream cheese or whatever is going. You could wash it all down with their malt beer, especially bottled for them in Belgium.

DRINK

MAUMAU UNDERGROUND *Club*

☎ 93 441 80 15; www.maumaunderground.com; Carrer de la Fontrodona 33; 11pm-2.30am Thu, to 3am Fri & Sat; M Paral.lel

Funk, soul, hip-hop – you never know what you might run into in this popular little Poble Sec music and dance haunt. Above the backlit bar a huge screen spews forth psychodelic images, which on Sunday afternoons (see website for hours) converts to a football screen for laid-back fans.

TINTA ROJA *Club*

☎ 93 443 32 43; Carrer de la Creu dels Molers 17; 8pm-1am Wed & Thu, to 3am Fri & Sat, 7pm-midnight Sun; M Poble Sec

You never quite know what might you might see in this tunnel-like space. Through a succession of spaces all suffused with reddish light, you penetrate to an area where anything could happen, from theatre to tango or acrobatics. The hushed atmosphere is always pleasant for a tipple.

PLAY

PISCINES BERNAT PICORNELL *Gym*

☎ 93 423 40 41; www.picornell.com; Avinguda de l'Estadi 30-40; adult over 25yr/senior & child 6-14yr/youth 15-25yr €8.50/4.50/5.60, outdoor pool only Jun-Sep adult/senior & child 6-14yr €4.50/3.20; 7am-midnight Mon-Fri, to 9pm Sat, 7.30am-4pm Sun, outdoor pool 10am-7pm Mon-Sat, to 4pm Sun Oct-May, 9am-9pm Mon-Sat, to 8pm Sun Jun-Sep;

Included in the standard admission price to Barcelona's official Olympic pool on Montjuïc is use of the gym, saunas and spa bath.

SALA APOLO
Live Music & Club

☎ 93 441 40 01; www.sala-apolo.com; Carrer Nou de la Rambla 113, Poble Sec; admission €6-12; 12.30am-5am Wed-Sat, 10.30pm-3.30am Sun; M Paral.lel

This former music hall is the scene of a fiery and eclectic dance and concert scene. Gigs (often starting about 9pm) range from world music to touring rock bands you'll never again see in a venue so cosy. After the encores, the hall is cleared for Nitsaclub (a DJ team playing house, electro, neo-trance and more) on Friday and Saturday, Powderroom DJs on Thursday and a mix other nights.

TABLAO DE CARMEN
Flamenco

☎ 93 325 68 95; www.tablaodecarmen.com; Carrer dels Arcs 9, Poble Espanyol; show only €31, dinner & show €59; shows 9.30pm & 11.30pm Tue-Sun; M Espanya

Named after the great Barcelonin *bailaora* (flamenco dancer) Carmen Amaya, this place features a lively show with a full cast of guitarists, singers and dancers. Touristy, but not as bad as might be expected.

TEATRE LLUIRE *Theatre*

☎ 93 289 27 70; www.teatrelliure.com; Passeig de Santa Madrona 3; admission €10-20; box office 5-8pm; M Espanya; ♿

With two spaces (Espai Lliure and Sala Fabià Puigserver), the Free Theatre hosts a variety of quality drama, almost exclusively in Catalan. There are occasional local international acts, including modern dance and music. A restaurant and bar makes a night out here easy.

TERRRAZZA *Club*

☎ 93 423 12 85; www.laterrrazza.com; Avinguda del Marquès de Comillas, Poble Espanyol; admission €18; midnight-7am Fri & Sat May-Oct; M Espanya

Some of the biggest international names play at this summertime must, which can be relied on for a range of the meatiest house, techno-trance and pop-rock on vinyl, and a clientele of extremely high-quality eye candy. Move to 'the terrace' for rejuvenation when you run out of steam. In winter the club moves indoors and becomes Discothèque.

WATERWORKS IN THE ALTOGETHER

You can get all your gear off year-round at the Piscines Bernat Picornell (see opposite), the Olympic pool on Montjuïc. On Saturday, between 9pm and 11pm, the pool (with access to sauna and steam bath) is open only to nudists (adult/child & senior €4.50/3.20). On Sunday from October to May the indoor pool is also for nudists only, from 4.15pm to 6pm.

>SNAPSHOTS

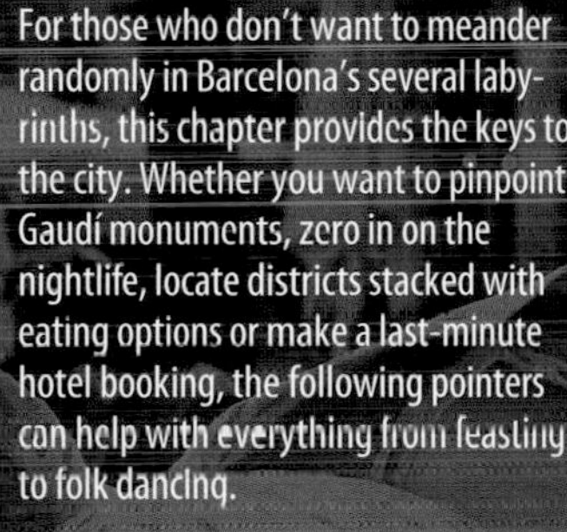

For those who don't want to meander randomly in Barcelona's several labyrinths, this chapter provides the keys to the city. Whether you want to pinpoint Gaudí monuments, zero in on the nightlife, locate districts stacked with eating options or make a last-minute hotel booking, the following pointers can help with everything from feasting to folk dancing.

Capgrossos (dwarves with big heads) during Festes de la Mercè celebrations (p36)

ACCOMMODATION

Hotel construction in Barcelona continues apace, just as the city continues to register high occupation rates. It can get tight when trade fairs are on (which is a lot of the time), so booking is warmly recommended. The city is compact, so wherever you choose to stay you will never be too far from the action.

The Barri Gòtic, especially on and around La Rambla and Carrer de Ferran, is jammed with mostly cheapish *hostales,* and generally attracts a boisterous, young, budget crowd. A similar tale applies to El Raval. There are some notable high-end exceptions (some recommended in the boxed text opposite). The single biggest disadvantage of many of these places can be nocturnal street noise as revellers fill the night air with their rocket-fuelled cheer.

Surprisingly, only a handful of options dot the busy La Ribera district or the waterfront. The exception is the El Fòrum area, at the city's extreme northeast, where midrange and luxury hotels have sprung up to cater to the conference crowd – when that crowd isn't around, prices in these near-new establishments tend to tumble. You are about 20 minutes from the city centre by Metro, but near the sea.

All sorts of hotels are scattered across L'Eixample. This is an extensive area and, depending on what you choose, you will either be just a short stroll outside the Old City centre or several Metro stops away. You might decide to take a room in a slightly fusty, old-style *pensión* or *hostal* (small-scale hotels) along Rambla de Catalunya or opt for a bright, new, modern midrange number or a luxury location with a rooftop pool and gourmet restaurant.

Need a place to stay? Find and book it at lonelyplanet .com. More than 50 properties are featured for Barcelona – each personally visited, thoroughly reviewed and happily recommended by a Lonely Planet author. From hostels to high-end hotels, we've hunted out the places that will bring you unique and special experiences. Read independent reviews by authors and other travel aficionados like you, and get practical information including amenities, maps and photos. Then reserve your room simply and securely via Haystack - our online booking service. It's all at www.lonelyplanet.com/accommodation.

A good website for seeking out some of the city's more striking hotels is **Barcelona Selection** (www.barcelona-selection.com). Otherwise, book on the city's tourism office site (www.barcelonaturisme.com).

An increasingly popular option is short-term apartment rentals. Agencies and websites offering these abound. They include **Barcelona Online** (www.barcelona-on-line.es); **Barcelona Apartments** (www.barcelona partments.com); **Apartment Barcelona** (www.apartmentbarcelona.com) and **Lodging Barcelona** (www.lodgingbarcelona.com).

BEST FOR VIEWS & POOLS

> Hotel Arts Barcelona (www.ritzcarlton.com)
> Hotel Barcelona Princess (www.hotelbarcelonaprincess.com)
> Hotel Rey Juan Carlos I (www.hrjuancarlos.com)
> Gran Hotel La Florida (www.hotellaflorida.com)
> Grand Marina Hotel (www.grandmarinahotel.com)

BEST FOR LOWER BUDGETS

> Hotel d'Uxelles (www.hotelduxelles.com)
> Hostal Palacios (www.hostalpalacios.com)
> Pensió 2000 (www.pensio2000.com)
> Hostal Gat Xino (www.gataccommodation.com)
> Hostal Goya (www.hostalgoya.com)
> Sea Point Hostel (www.seapointhostel.com)
> Centric Point Hostel (www.centricpointhostel.com)
> Alberg Mare de Déu de Montserrat (www.tujuca.com)

BEST FOR DESIGN

> Hotel Omm (www.hotelomm.es)
> Hotel Banys Orientals (www.hotelbanysorientals.com)
> Hotel Claris (www.derbyhotels.es)
> Casa Camper (www.camper.com)
> Hotel Prestige (www.prestigepaseodegracia.com)
> Market Hotel (www.markethotel.com.es)
> Grand Hotel Central (www.grandhotelcentral.com)

BEST FOR HISTORY

> Hotel Neri (www.hotelneri.com)
> Hotel 1898 (www.nnhotels.es)
> Hotel Palace (www.hotelpalacebarcelona.com)
> Hotel San Agustín (www.hotelsa.com)
> Hotel Gran Via (www.nnhotels.es)
> Chic & Basic (www.chicandbasic.com)

BEST FOR MODERNISTA TOUCHES

> Hotel Casa Fuster (www.hotelcasafuster.com)
> Hotel Mesón de Castilla (www.husa.es)

SHOPPING

For high fashion, design, jewellery and many department stores, the main shopping axis starts on Plaça de Catalunya, proceeds up Passeig de Gràcia and turns left (west) into Avinguda Diagonal, along which it proceeds as far as Plaça de la Reina Maria Cristina. The densely packed section between Plaça de Francesc Macià (Map p133, D4) and Plaça de la Reina Maria Cristina (Map p133, C4) in Zona Alta is an especially good hunting ground.

The heart of L'Eixample – known as the Quadrat d'Or (Golden Square) – is jammed with all sorts of glittering shops. La Rambla de Catalunya (Map pp104–5, C4) is lined with chic stores, Carrer del Consell de Cent (Map pp104–5, D4) bursts with art galleries and the nearby streets are also busy with shopping options, from specialist wine boutiques to high fashion.

The heart of the Barri Gòtic has come crackling to life since the mid-1990s, and local shopkeepers like to think of the whole area as 'Barnacentre' (from Barna – slang for Barcelona). Some of the most curious old stores, whether purveyors of hats or of candles, lurk in the narrow lanes around Plaça de Sant Jaume (Map p47, C3). The once-seedy Carrer d'Avinyó (Map p47, D4) has become a minor fashion boulevard, with creations by up-and-coming designers for a young (and young at heart) clientele. Antique stores abound on and around Carrer de la Palla (Map p47, B2) and Carrer dels Banys Nous (Map p47, B3).

Over in La Ribera there are two categories of shops to look out for: some fine old traditional stores dealing in speciality foodstuffs, and a new crop of fashion and design stores (particularly along the stretch of Carrer del Rec between Passeig del Born and Avinguda del Marquès de l'Argentera, Map pp76–7, E4) catering to the young professionals who have moved into the *barri*. Old-time stores abound in El Raval, where you'll also discover a cluster of preloved clothes shops on Carrer de la Riera Baixa (Map p65, B4).

Most places have retail windows between 10am and 2pm and 4pm and 8pm. Traditional and most smaller shops observe the siesta, while the modern ones (such as fashion stores, and major book and record stores), and many on main shopping boulevards, often stay open throughout the day. Department stores such as El Corte Inglés and other major shops tend to open from around 10am to 10pm Monday to Saturday. Virtually all shops are closed on Sunday and some of the smaller ones close on Monday morning. In July, August and in some cases September, many stores adopt 'summer hours', which can mean anything but generally involves later morning starts, shorter hours and closing on Saturday.

Non-EU residents are entitled to a refund of the 16% IVA on purchases of more than €90.16 from any shop if they take the goods out of the EU within three months. Ask the shop for a Cashback (or similar) refund form, which you present (with goods, prior to check-in) at the customs booth for IVA refunds when you leave Spain. At Barcelona airport, look for the customs booth opposite the bar on the ground floor of Terminal A.

WHERE FOODIES GO TO HEAVEN

> Caelum (p54)
> Escribà (p55)
> Casa Gispert (p81)
> El Magnífico (p83)
> La Botifarreria (p83)
> Vila Viniteca (p84)
> Mas Bacus (p117)

MADE FOR WALKING

> Camper (p114)
> Farrutx (p114)

WORDS & SOUNDS

> Antinous (p53)
> Altaïr (p113)
> Casa del Llibre (p114)
> Laie (p116)
> Castelló (p68)
> Etnomusic (p68)

Top left Upmarket shoppers on Passeig de Gràcia

FASHION

Barcelona's shopping streets are dripping with international and Spanish (Zara, Adolfo Domínguez, Massimo Dutti and many more) brand stars. But the city is also home to many of its own top designers. *Prêt-à-porter* giant Mango is a Barcelona success story. Emerging as one of the hippest local names on the world fashion catwalks is the youthful Custo Barcelona, with a rapidly growing chain of stores in Spain and abroad.

Other local names or Barcelona-based designers include Antonio Miró, Joaquim Verdú, David Valls, Josep Font, Armand Basi, Purificación García, Konrad Muhr, Sita Murt and TCN. Happily, prices for both international and local designer clothing is often much lower than in cities such as London.

Good and bad news characterised the local fashion scene in 2006. Early in the year, the regional government dropped funding for the annual Barcelona high-fashion show, the Pasarela Gaudí, leaving the way open to Madrid to dominate the Spanish scene with its Pasarela Cibeles. Then in October, the successful German urban street-wear show Bread & Butter announced it was dropping its Berlin gig in favour of Barcelona, where it had staged an annual repeat festival since 2005! Swings and roundabouts.

FIXATED ON FASHION

> Custo Barcelona (p81)
> Antonio Miró (p113)
> Armand Basi (p113)
> Josep Font (p116)
> Mango (p116)
> Zara (p118)

PUBLIC ART

The streets, squares and parks of Barcelona are littered with the signatures of artists past and present, famous and unknown. Since the return of democracy in the late 1970s, the town hall has not been shy about encouraging the placement of sometimes grandiose and often equally incomprehensible contemporary works in the city's public space. Reactions range from admiration to perplexity. Justly proud of its rich street art heritage, the council has also created an extensive archive of it all on the internet at www.bcn.es. Click on Art Públic.

The best thing about art in the streets is that it is open to all comers. Of the many hundreds of statues and other works around town, we list some outstanding pieces here.

FREE FOR ALL

> *Barcelona Head* (p92; pictured above)
> *David i Goliat* (p98)
> *Dona i Ocell* (p138)
> *El Desconsol* (p81)
> *Gat* (p66)
> *Homenatge a la Barceloneta* (p89)

ARCHITECTURE

For some, Barcelona is a party town, but many come for its rich and varied architectural heritage. Gaudí and the Modernistas, long scorned by the locals, have become universal favourites. To enjoy their whimsy, you will want to explore L'Eixample, the city's grid-plan district where most of the Modernista building was undertaken. Less well known is the city's Gothic heritage, to be admired mostly in the Barri Gòtic and La Ribera. The city is not shy of dotting the skyline with daring new structures. Several have been added in the past few years and more are in the pipeline. For more on the background to Barcelona's architecture, see p179; for details on a Modernisme pack offering a discount on the main Modernista buildings in town, see p107.

BEST OF GAUDÍ

> La Pedrera (p109)
> Casa Batlló (see Manzana de la Discordia, p103)
> La Sagrada Família (p109)
> Palau Güell (p67)
> Park Güell (p128)

GOOD NEW LOOKERS

> Torre Agbar by Jean Nouvel (p98)
> Mercat de Santa Caterina by Enric Miralles (p75)
> Macba by Richard Meier (p66)
> Edifici Fòrum by Herzog & de Meuron (p98)
> Edifici de Gas Natural by Enric Miralles (p89)
> Teatre Nacional de Catalunya by Ricard Bofill (p125)

GOTHIC GREATNESS

> Església de Santa Maria del Mar (p75)
> Museu Marítim (p93)
> Saló del Tinell/Museu d'Història de la Ciutat (p50)
> Museu-Monestir de Pedralbes (p135)
> Museu Picasso (p79)
> La Catedral (p49)

MORE MODERNISME

> Palau de la Música by Lluís Domènech i Montaner (p79)
> Casa Amatller by Josep Puig i Cadafalch (see Manzana de la Discordia, p110)
> Hospital de la Santa Creu i de Sant Pau by Lluís Domènech i Montaner (p107)
> Palau del Baró Quadras – Casa Asia by Josep Puig i Cadafalch (p112)

PAINTING

Three of the great names in 20th-century art are associated with Barcelona and two left behind considerable legacies in the city. Art museums dedicated to Pablo Picasso and Joan Miró are among the most popular sights in the city. Having admired early Picasso and the breadth of Miró's work in Barcelona, it would be a shame to miss the loopiness of that doyen of daftness, Salvador Dalí.

To enjoy the full impact of Dalí's work, you need to invest in a train ride north to Figueres. He dubbed his **Teatre-Museu Dalí** (☎ 972 67 75 00; www.salvador-dali.org; Plaça de Gala i Salvador Dalí; adult/student €10/7, summer nights €11; 9am-7.45pm Jul-Sep, 10.30am-5.45pm Tue-Sun Oct-Jun, summer nights 10pm-1am Aug) the spiritual centre of Europe. Make of that what you will, but his zany museum-mausoleum certainly put his otherwise dull, provincial birthplace, Figueres, on the map. It comprises three floors of tricks, illusions and absurdity, along with plenty of Dalí's inimitable art. A separate section is Dalí Joies, showcasing exquisite jewellery designed by the master. (For train timetables and prices from Barcelona to Figueres, check www.renfe.es.)

Possibly the single greatest assembly of Romanesque art can be seen in the magnificent Museu Nacional d'Art de Catalunya (MNAC) in Montjuïc, along with collections of Gothic and Modernista and other art, Catalan and European, from down the centuries. Smaller collections are worth checking out too. For contemporary art, the headline museum is the Museu d'Art Contemporani de Barcelona (Macba; p66). For more details on Barcelona's artists, see p181.

ART FOR ART'S SAKE

For a selection of Tàpies' works and contemporary art exhibitions Fundació Antoni Tàpies (p107)
For Joan Miró Fundació Joan Miró (p143)
For a private and eclectic art collection Fundación Francisco Godia (p107)
For international contemporary art Museu d'Art Contemporani de Barcelona (Macba; p66)
For a modest collection of ancient Egyptian art Museu Egipci (p112)
For Romanesque sculpture Museu Frederic Marès (p51)
For the gamut of Catalan art Museu Nacional d'Art de Catalunya (MNAC; p148)
For early Picasso Museu Picasso (p79)

FLAMENCO

The stirring sounds of flamenco, a cultural hybrid mixing the music of *gitanos* (Roma) with other influences (from North African Berber music to Gregorian chants and traditional medieval Jewish music), is usually associated with Andalucía in southern Spain. But the *gitanos* who arrived in Spain from India in the Middle Ages were also present in Catalonia. Records of *gitanos* performing in Barcelona date from the 19th century, when the music came to prominence across the country. Perhaps the best-known flamenco dancer born in Catalonia and associated with Barcelona was Carmen Amaya (1913–63). In the 1950s, Antonio Gonzáles 'El Pescailla' and Peret were among those behind the Rumba Catalana, a surge of Catalan flamenco with musical influences from the Americas. For more on flamenco in Barcelona see www.flamencobarcelona.com. Listed here are some names in contemporary Catalan flamenco worth looking out for.

CATALAN FIRE

> Duquende
> Miquel Poveda
> Ginesa Ortega
> Montse Cortes
> Mayte Martín

SARDANA

Catalans take their national dance, the *sardana,* seriously (it is not a dance accompanied by peals of laughter). Dancers gather to form a circle, usually piling up their bags and other chattels in the middle. All hold hands and execute a series of complex steps, bobbing up and down and heading right and left.

The accompanying music, by turns melancholic and jolly, is played by a reed-and-brass band called a *cobla,* and most of it was written by the 19th century. The origins of the dance are unclear, but the first written reference appeared in the 16th century. Popular assurances that the *sardana* was banned under Franco are hotly disputed by those who have taken the trouble to study the period.

Even many Catalans will quietly confess they are not great fans of this folk dancing, but as an affirmation of Catalan identity it has its own particular charm. And many seem to genuinely enjoy it.

Sardanas are danced at traditional festivals, but the most likely chance you'll have of seeing them is in front of **La Catedral** (p49; 7pm Wed, 6.30-8.30pm Sat, noon-2pm Sun).

CATALAN CUISINE

Sure, Barcelona has become a cauldron of culinary kookiness, with the foams and froths of master chef Ferran Adrià and his acolytes. But you can still get a taste of yesteryear and traditional Catalan cooking.

Rice is grown in the Delta de l'Ebre area in southern Catalonia and used widely. *Arròs a la cassola* or *arròs a la catalana* is Catalan paella, cooked in an earthenware pot and without saffron, whereas *arròs negre* is rice cooked in cuttlefish ink – much tastier than it sounds. *Fideuá* is similar to paella, but uses noodles rather than rice. You should also receive a little side dish of *allioli* (a mayonnaise-style sauce of pounded garlic with olive oil) to mix in.

Seafood is high on Catalan menus, but hearty meat dishes from the interior also figure prominently on many menus. *Botifarra* (sausages) come in many shapes and sizes, and for some there's nothing better than a sizzling *solomillo* (sirloin) prepared *a punto* (medium rare).

Catalans are passionate about *calçots* (large, sweet spring onions), which are roasted over hot coals, dipped in spicy *romesco* sauce (a finely ground mixture of tomatoes, peppers, onions, garlic, almonds and olive oil) and eaten voraciously when in season from January until March.

Traditional desserts include *crema Catalana,* a delicious version of *crème brûlée*, but you might also be offered *mel i mató,* honey and fresh cream cheese.

GOOD OLD-FASHIONED COOKING

> Casa Leopoldo (p69)
> Suquet de l'Almirall (p94)
> Agut (p57)
> Bilbao (p129)
> Cafè de l'Acadèmia (p57)

CAFÉS & RESTAURANTS

Catalans love eating and they love style. In Barcelona, new restaurants and cafés open (and close) with astounding rapidity, although brand spanking new is not always synonymous with good. Never fear, for the choice of good places is overwhelming!

A few old-guard restaurants specialise in traditional Catalan cooking, while other equally venerable establishments, often run by Basques or Galicians, offer a mix of their regional specialities and what can loosely be termed 'Spanish cooking'. Such places are scattered across the Barri Gòtic, El Raval and L'Eixample areas. Seafood is also prominent, especially in La Barceloneta.

Catalans eat late and, often, they eat big: most have three or even four courses for lunch (between 2pm and 4pm), and nobody sits down for dinner much before 9.30pm. Booking is advisable at midrange and expensive places, especially from Thursday to Saturday.

BEST FOR PAELLA

> Palau de Mar (p95)
> Elche (p149)
> Set (7) Portes (p86)
> Restaurant Pitarra (p60)

BEST FOR DEALS & DINNERS

> Casa Calvet (p119; pictured right)
> Ca l'Isidre (p69)
> Casa Darío (p119)
> Hofmann (p85)
> Agut (p57)

BEST FOR VEGETARIAN OPTIONS

> Biocenter (p69)
> Sesamo (p70)
> Amaltea (p119)
> La Flauta Mágica (p85)

NIGHTLIFE

Barcelona knows how to party, but to experience the city in its natural light you'll need to go out late. Barcelonins are still in front of the mirror by the time you're usually in full flight, bars are barely getting into their stride at 10pm and clubs (best on Thursday to Saturday nights) don't come alive before 2am.

The lower end of the Barri Gòtic, the hip El Born area and parts of El Raval (where you'll find the bulk of the city's truly atmospheric old bars, some with a century of history) are all busy, with bars of all descriptions. In L'Eixample, the main axis is along Carrer d'Aribau (Map pp104-5, B4) and into the chichi Zona Alta area around Carrer de Tuset and Carrer de Marià Cubí (Map p133, D4). The squares and some streets of Gràcia also hop.

In the Old City labyrinth lurks a surprising variety of clubs. On the waterfront, a sun-scorched crowd of visiting yachties mixes it up with tourists and a few locals at noisy dance bars. Class, they will tell you, is reserved for L'Eixample and Zona Alta.

Check out *Guía del Ocio* (www.guiadelociobcn.es; €1; available from newsstands), *Micro, Go Mag* and *Salir* (all in Spanish; free from bars) and Barceloca (www.barceloca.com) and BCN-Nightlife (www.bcn-nightlife .com) for more information.

TIPPLING WITH HISTORY
> Bar Marsella (p70)
> London Bar (p73)
> Casa Almirall (p72)
> Bar Muy Buenas (p71)
> Bar Pastís (p71)

SIPPING WITH STYLE
> Dry Martini (p122)
> Gimlet (p87)
> Hotel Omm Bar (p123)

BEST CLUBS
> Otto Zutz (p141)
> Terrrazza (p151)
> La Paloma (p73; pictured right)
> Sutton Club (p141)

TAPAS

Today's emblematic Spanish bar snacks supposedly originated in Andalucía's sherry area in the 19th century, when bar owners placed a piece of bread on top of a drink to deter flies; this developed into the custom of putting a titbit, such as olives or a piece of sausage, on a lid to cover the drink – something salty to encourage drinking. Since then, tapas have become a cuisine of their own. Not an integral part of Catalan eating tradition, tapas culture was long ago imported to Barcelona. Particularly popular are the Basque Country versions, *pintxos,* which come in the form of little canapés. On slices of baguette are perched anything from *bacalao* (deep-fried cod) to *morcilla* (black pudding). In some gourmet spots, tapas have become something of an art form, while in many straightforward, beery bars you might just get a saucer of olives to accompany your tipple.

TAPAS TIME

> Cal Pep (p84)
> Taktika Berri (p121)
> El Vaso de Oro (p94)
> Inopia (p120)
> Cerveseria Catalana (p120)
> Quimet i Quimet (p150)

BULLFIGHTING

In 2004 the city council narrowly voted for a symbolic declaration that Barcelona was anti-bullfighting. Animal rights groups and many Catalans, who consider *la lidia* (bullfighting) a cultural imposition from Spain, were delighted. The vote was divisive because, like it or not, bullfighting has a long history in Barcelona.

Bullfighting is by no means an exclusively Castilian (central Spanish) activity. It has a long history in Portugal and southern France, too, and indeed spectacles involving bull-baiting in one form or another were common in other parts of Europe and were rooted in the legacy of such 'games' under the Roman Empire.

The first bullfight in Barcelona was held in 1387, long before Catalonia was subordinated to Castilian overlordship. And Catalans may or may not be less enthusiastic about bullfighting than other Spaniards (vegetarian anarchists banned it during the civil war in Barcelona), but this doesn't stop them from staging a season at the Plaça de Braus Monumental bullring (Map pp104–5, G2) on the corner of Carrer de la Marina and Gran Via de les Corts Catalanes, usually on Sundays in spring and summer. Local *toreros* include Manolo Porcel and Serafín Marin. Occasional performances at the bullring by the big-name bullfighters listed here are major events.

STARS OF THE RING

> Julián 'El Juli' López
> 'Joselito' (José Miguel Arroyo)
> Manuel Jesús 'El Cid'
> David Fandila 'El Fandi'
> El Cordobés (Manuel Díaz)

FOOTBALL

Football has something of the status of religion in Barcelona. Indeed, in this traditionally rose-tinged town (with a serious conservative overlay in its entrepreneurial class), one is tempted to see the Camp Nou football stadium (see the boxed text, p134) as the principal temple of worship. The object of such ecstasy is Football Club Barcelona (www.fcbarcelona.com), one of the most exciting teams in Europe and bastion of Catalan identity (in spite of the majority of players being from abroad). After a few years in the doldrums, FC Barcelona has been in crackling form since winning the 2004–05 premiership. It all started on 29 November 1899, when Swiss Hans Gamper founded FC Barcelona (Barça) four years after English residents had first played the game here. His choice of club colours, the blue and maroon of his home town, Winterthur, have stuck. Barça is one of only three teams (Real Madrid and Athletic de Bilbao) never to have been relegated to the 2nd division.

The city's other club, Espanyol (www.rcdespanyol.com), based at the **Estadi Olímpic** (Map pp144-5, E4; Avinguda de l'Estadi; 🚌 50, 61 & PM), traditionally plays a quiet second fiddle to Barça.

BEACHES

Barcelona's reputation as a metropolitan seaside resort is fully justified and yet totally artificial. That is, the beaches are artificial. Every year winter storms sweep away tonnes of sand from these largely manmade beaches, and the town council patiently replaces it.

Starting from the southwestern end of town, Platja de Sant Miquel is, from the mid-afternoon, a bit of a gay-male nudist strip, although very relaxed. Platja de Sant Sebastià and Platja de la Barceloneta are more family affairs. The five beaches stretching northeast from Port Olímpic (starting with Platja de Nova Icària) have nicer (less muddy-seeming) sand and cleaner water. All have at least one *chiringuito,* snacks and drinks bars that set up on the beaches and often open until 1am (Easter to October).

Those hankering for beaches outside town are spoiled for choice and limited only by transport options and time. Northeast of the city, the train to Blanes zips past beach after beach along the Costa del Maresme. Some have an urban flavour, others are more tucked away. The sand is sandier and the water noticeably more transparent the further you get from the city. Then follows the Costa Brava, most easily accessible with your own wheels.

To the southwest, the beaches of the Costa del Garraf and then the Costa Daurada tend to be broad, flat affairs. The further south you head, the less chance of encountering even a speck of cloud. Apart from Torredembarra, Platja d'Altafulla and Cala de la Mora (for which you'll need your own transport), these beaches can all be reached by train.

OUR FAVOURITES ON THE COSTA DEL MARESME

> Caldes d'Estrac
> Arenys de Mar
> Canet de Mar
> Sant Pol de Mar
> Platja dels Pins (Malgrat de Mar)

OUR FAVOURITES ON THE COSTA DEL GARRAF & COSTA DAURADA

> Garraf
> Sitges
> Cubelles
> Torredembarra
> Platja d'Altafulla
> Cala de la Mora (Tamarit)

KIDS IN BARCELONA

In summer especially kids will love Barcelona's beaches, pools and parks. Quite a few of the sights are bound to fascinate them, too, and the sheer theatre of central Barcelona's streets will keep them agog.

Most of the mid- and upper-range hotels in Barcelona can organise a babysitting service. A company that many hotels use and that you can also contact directly is **5 Serveis** (☎ 93 412 56 76, 639 361111; Carrer de Pelai 50). It has multilingual babysitters *(canguros)*. Rates vary, but in the evening expect to pay around €7.50 an hour plus the cost of a taxi home for the babysitter.

Tender Loving Canguros (☎ 647 605989, www.tlcanguros.com) offers English-speaking babysitters for a minimum of three hours (€7 an hour).

The listed sights should please most kids of most ages.

TOPS FOR KIDS

> L'Aquàrium (p89)
> Beaches (opposite)
> Parc del Fòrum & Zona de Banys (p98)
> Parc d'Atraccions (p136)
> CosmoCaixa (p134)
> Zoo de Barcelona (p80)
> Poble Espanyol (p149)
> Transbordador c (p93)
> Golondrina boat tours (p89)
> Parc de la Ciutadella (p80)

GAY & LESBIAN BARCELONA

Barcelona has a busy gay scene, as does Sitges on the coast to the southwest. In Barcelona, the bulk of the action happens in an area about five to six blocks southwest of Passeig de Gràcia around Carrer de Consell de Cent (Map pp104–5, D4). Sitges (p110), meanwhile, attracts an international gay crowd from Easter to the tail end of summer, and comes to life with a bang for Carnaval (Carnival) in February, when it puts on outrageous parades around the centre of town.

The age of consent in Spain (for both homosexuals and heterosexuals) is 12 years. Same-sex marriages were legalised in 2005, and a Catalan gay couple became the first in Spain to legally adopt a child in mid-2006.

Casal Lambda (Map pp76-7, B3; ☎ 93 319 55 50; www.lambdaweb.org; Carrer de Verdaguer i Callis 10; Ⓜ Urquinaona) is a gay and lesbian social centre. The **Coordinadora Gai-Lesbiana** (Map pp144-5, B1; ☎ in Spain 902 120140, from abroad 93 298 10 88; www.cogailes.org; Carrer de Finlàndia 45; Ⓜ Plaça de Sants) is the city's main coordinating body for gay and lesbian groups.

GayBarcelona.Net (www.gaybarcelona.net in Spanish) has news and views and an extensive listings section covering bars, saunas, shops and more in Barcelona and Sitges.

BEST GAY BARS & CLUBS

> Aire (p122)
> Dietrich Gay Teatro Café (p122)
> Arena Madre (p123)
> Metro (p124)
> New Chaps (p124)
> Salvation (p125)

BEST GAY STAYS

> Hotel Axel (www.axelhotels.com)
> Hotel California (www.hotelcalifornia bcn.com)

>BACKGROUND

Temple del Sagrat Cor, Tibidabo (p32)

BACKGROUND

HISTORY

WILFRED THE HAIRY & MEDITERRANEAN EXPANSION

The Romans put Barcino on the map in the 3rd century BC and were later followed by the Visigoths, Moors and Franks who, in the 9th century AD, put it under the control of local counts as a buffer zone against Muslim-dominated Spain.

Count Guifré el Pelós (Wilfred the Hairy) wrested control over several neighbouring territories in what later became known as Catalonia, and by 878 Barcelona was its key city. He founded a dynasty that lasted nearly five centuries. After the Franks failed to help Barcelona repel a Muslim assault in 985, the region became independent of Frankish suzerainty.

The counts of Barcelona gradually expanded their territory south, expelling the Muslims from what is now southern Catalonia. In 1137 Ramon Berenguer IV, the count of Barcelona, married Petronilla, heiress to the throne of neighbouring Aragón, and thus created the combined Crown of Aragón. In the following centuries the regime became a flourishing merchant empire, seizing Valencia and the Balearic Islands from the Muslims and later taking territories as far flung as Sardinia, Sicily and parts of Greece.

CASTILIAN DOMINANCE

Overstretched, racked by civil disobedience and decimated by the Black Death, Catalonia began to wobble by the 14th century. When the last count of Wilfred the Hairy's dynasty expired without leaving an heir,

ROUGH JUSTICE

Medieval Catalonia developed its own system of laws, the Usatges, based on Roman-Visigothic precepts and feudal custom in the 11th century. It could be a little rough: '...let them (the rulers) render justice as it seems fit to them: by cutting off hands and feet, putting out eyes, keeping men in prison for a long time and, ultimately, in hanging their bodies if necessary... In regard to women, let the rulers render justice by cutting off their noses, lips, ears and breasts, and by burning them at the stake if necessary...' One wonders what the definition of necessary was.

the Crown of Aragón was passed to a noble of Castile. Soon these two Spanish kingdoms merged, with Catalonia left as a very junior partner. As business shifted from the Mediterranean to the Atlantic after the discovery of the Americas in 1492, Catalans were increasingly marginalised from trade.

The region, which had retained some autonomy in the running of its own affairs, was dealt a crushing blow when it supported the wrong side in the War of the Spanish Succession (1702–13) and the Bourbon king Felipe V established a unitary Castilian state. He banned the writing and teaching of Catalan, swept away the remnants of local legal systems and tore down a whole district of medieval Barcelona in order to construct an immense fort (on the site of the present-day Parc de la Ciutadella, p80), whose sole purpose was to watch over Barcelona's troublemakers.

ECONOMIC GROWTH & THE RENAIXENÇA

Buoyed by the lifting of the ban on its trade with the Americas in 1778, Barcelona embarked on the road to industrial revolution, based initially on textiles but spreading to wine, cork and iron in the mid 19th century. It soon became Spain's leading city. As the economy prospered, Barcelona outgrew its medieval walls, which were demolished in 1854. Work on the grid plan L'Eixample (the Extension) district began soon after. The so-called Renaixença (Renaissance) brought a revival of Catalan culture, as well as political activism, and sowed the seeds of growing political tension in the early 20th century as demands for autonomy from the central state became more insistent.

ANARCHY, CIVIL WAR & FRANCO

Adding to the fiery mix was growing discontent among the working class. The grand Catalan merchant-bourgeois families grew richer, displaying their wealth in a slew of whimsical private mansions built with verve and flair by Modernista (Catalan Art Nouveau) architects such as Antoni Gaudí. At the same time, the industrial working class, housed in cramped quarters such La Barceloneta and El Raval and oppressed by poverty and disease, became organised and on occasion violent. Spain's neutrality during WWI had boosted Barcelona's economy, and from 1900 to 1930 the population doubled to one million, but the postwar global slump hit the city hard. Waves of strikes, organised principally by the anarchists' Confederación Nacional del Trabajo (CNT), brought tough responses. Left-wing and right-wing gangs took their ideological conflict to the streets. Tit-for-tat assassinations became common currency and the death toll mounted.

When the Second Spanish Republic was created under a left-wing government in 1931, Catalonia declared independence. Later, under pressure, its leaders settled for devolution, which it then lost in 1934, when a right-wing government won power in Madrid. The election of a left-wing popular front in 1936 again sparked Catalan autonomy claims but also led General Franco to launch the Spanish Civil War (1936–39), from which he emerged the victor. Barcelona, which for much of the war was the acting capital of Spain, was regularly bombed from March 1938 on, mostly by Fascist Italian aircraft based in Franco-occupied Mallorca.

Barcelona was run by anarchists and the Partido Obrero de Unificación Marxista (POUM; the Marxist Unification Workers' Party) Trotskyist militia until mid-1937. Unions took over factories and public services, hotels and mansions became hospitals and schools, everyone wore workers' clothes, bars and cafés were collectivised, trams and taxis were painted red and black (the colours of the anarchists) and one-way streets were ignored as they were seen to be part of the old system.

The more radical anarchists were behind the burning of most of the city's churches and the shooting of more than 1200 priests, monks and nuns. The anarchists in turn were shunted aside by the communists (directed by Stalin from Moscow) after a bloody internecine battle in Barcelona that left 1500 dead in May 1937.

The Republican defeat at the hands of the Nationalists in the Battle of the Ebro in southern Catalonia in summer 1938 left Barcelona undefended. It fell to the Nationalists on 25 January 1939. Purges and executions under Franco continued until well into the 1950s.

THE CITY REBORN

The Francoist Josep Maria de Porcioles was mayor from 1957 until his death in 1973, a grey time for Barcelona marked by regular demonstrations against the regime, always brutally put down. When Franco himself died two years later, the city rejoiced. In 1977 Catalonia was granted regional autonomy.

The 1992 Olympics marked the beginning of a long process of urban renewal. The waterfront, beaches and Montjuïc were in the first wave, but the momentum hasn't been lost since. The Old City continues to be spruced up, and a determined campaign to repair the city's façades is lending Barcelona a brighter feel. Ambitious projects like the 22@hi-tech zone in the once-industrial Poblenou district and the fancy Diagonal Mar waterfront development around the Parc del Fòrum at the northeastern tip of the city are just two examples of Barcelona's urban dynamism.

LIFE IN BARCELONA

Spain's second city, Barcelona counts 1.6 million inhabitants, with another 3.4 million crammed into the province around the city. The loosely defined 'greater Barcelona area' is home to about 4.5 million people.

While much of the rest of Catalonia is largely Catalan in identity, Barcelona is a mixed bag. Massive internal migration in the 1950s and '60s brought 1.5 million Spaniards from other parts of the country to the capital and surrounding areas. Many of those families still prefer to speak Spanish over Catalan today.

The more affluent parts of the city and some central districts retain a predominantly Catalan flavour, but things are changing. Rapidly

READING BARCELONA

- > *Barcelona*, Robert Hughes – A witty and passionate study by the stormy Australian art critic of the art, architecture and life of the city through history.
- > *Homage to Catalonia*, George Orwell – Orwell's classic account of the first half of the 1936–39 Spanish Civil War as he experienced it in Barcelona and on the front line in Catalonia.
- > *La Ciudad de los Prodigios* (The City of Marvels), Eduardo Mendoza – A surreal novel set in Barcelona from the Universal Exhibition of 1888 to the World Exhibition of 1929. Through the story of the ruthless rise to power of its main protagonist, Mendoza paints a broad picture of Barcelona society in this turbulent period.
- > *La Sombra del Viento* (The Shadow of the Wind), Carlos Ruiz Zafón – This engaging mystery plays out over several periods in Barcelona's 20th-century history and is fascinating for anyone who has spent time, or intends to, in the city.
- > *Plaça del Diamant* (The Time of the Doves), Mercè Rodoreda – A slow-moving classic follows the life of the city before, during and after the civil war, as seen through the eyes of a local woman born in the Gràcia area.

increasing immigration from abroad is altering the city's face. Almost 15% of the officially resident population are foreigners, and 35% live in Ciutat Vella (the Old City).

The overwhelming majority of new arrivals are South Americans, but there are also sizable contingents from Morocco and Pakistan (mostly living in El Raval), as well as Eastern Europe (especially Romania and Bulgaria) and China. Many are illegal *(clandestinos)*. Throw in a good number of arrivals from affluent northern European countries in search of the good life, and the mix is heady.

Nominally, most Catalans are Catholics, although one study says that more than half of young Catalans declare themselves to be nonreligious. Indeed, Barcelona's working class has, since the 19th century, always given the city a politically reddish, anticlerical hue.

GOVERNMENT & POLITICS

Barcelona's politicians were unusually busy in 2006. The first ever left-wing coalition regional government in Catalonia in post-Franco times, elected in 2003 under popular former mayor socialist Pasqual Maragall, fell victim to coalition squabbling after Maragall managed to wring greater autonomy from the central government in Madrid.

The new autonomy statute (Estatut) was confirmed by referendum in 2006, but Maragall was obliged to step down by his colleagues in the Partit Socialista de Catalunya (PSC), the Catalan branch of the national Partido Socialista Obrero Español (PSOE, Spanish Socialist Workers' Party). Considered by many to have been weak in his handling of the delicate three-party coalition (Tripartit) that kept him in power, Maragall was given little chance. The departure of one of his coalition allies in disagreement over the Estatut precipitated his fall and provided the PSC bosses with the chance to find a new, and they hoped, more effective leader.

His replacement, José Montilla, until then Industry Minister in Madrid, took on Artur Mas of the right-wing Catalan regional coalition party, Convergència i Unió (CiU) in elections in November 2006. Mas came out on top, but with insufficient seats to form a majority government and so began a period of complex talks to create a new coalition government. In the end, Mas was frustrated, as Montilla reformed the Tripartit.

CARVALHO ON THE CASE

Manuel Vázquez Montalbán (1939–2003) was one of Barcelona's most prolific and best-loved writers, whose subjects ranged from essays on his home city to books on Cuba's Fidel Castro. He is best known for his detective series, featuring Pepe Carvalho. This overweight, somewhat depressed, food-loving private eye trawls the darker side of Barcelona's streets, but always finds time for a good meal and copious tipples. Oh, and always gets his man. Several of these stories have been published in English, including *South Seas*, *Off Side* and *Murder in the Central Committee* (which is actually set outside Barcelona).

Things were busy in the Ajuntament (town hall) too. Traditionally a left-wing haven, the Ajuntament stands opposite the Generalitat (regional government) building, which has generally been home to more conservative elements, on Plaça de Sant Jaume. In a game of shuffleboard, longtime but increasingly unpopular socialist mayor Joan Clos (who had succeeded Maragall in 1997), was given the chance to skip facing the electorate in the next municipal polls in spring 2007 and was summoned to Madrid to replace Montilla as Industry Minister. Into his shoes stepped 41-year old Jordi Hereu, whose mettle has yet to be tested.

ARCHITECTURE

Leaving aside Antoni Gaudí for a second, Barcelona is one of Europe's great Gothic treasure chests, and it was largely from these jewels that Gaudí and Modernistas of the late 19th and early 20th centuries took their inspiration, adapting the old rules and techniques to fit their new ways of seeing and building.

Catalan Gothic followed its own unique course. Decoration was used more sparingly than elsewhere and, most significantly, Catalan builders championed breadth over height. Stunning examples of this style include the Palau Reial's Saló del Tinell (see the Museu d'Història de la Ciutat, p50), the Drassanes (the former shipyards that now house the Museu Marítim, see p24) and the glorious Església de Santa Maria del Mar (p16).

Modernisme emerged as a trend in Barcelona during the 1880s, the city's *belle époque*. While the name suggests a rejection of the old techniques, the pioneers of the style actually delved deep into the past for inspiration, absorbed everything they could and then ripped up the rule book.

For many, Modernisme is synonymous with the name Antoni Gaudí (1852–1926). His works (starting with the unfinished La Sagrada Família church, p10) are the most daring and well known, but he was by no means alone. Lluís Domènech i Montaner (1850–1923) and Josep Puig i Cadafalch (1867–1957) left a wealth of remarkable buildings across the city. They range from Domènech i Montaner's gorgeous Palau de la Música Catalana (p79) to Puig i Cadafalch's playful medieval Dutch-looking Casa Amatller (see Manzana de la Discordia, p110). The many differences between all their designs underline just how eclectic and individual the Modernisme movement was.

Contemporary Barcelona is proving no slouch either, and a slew of local and international architects continues to contribute daring new elements to the city's skyline. The most spectacular is Jean Nouvel's cucumber-shaped, multicoloured tower, the Torre Agbar (p98).

BARCELONA ON FILM

Surprisingly few good films have been set in Barcelona, although a few more have been at least partially shot there. Among the best are the following:

> *Todo Sobre Mi Madre* (All About My Mother), Pedro Almodóvar (1999) – One of the Spanish director's most polished films, partly set in Barcelona. A quirky commentary that ties together the lives of the most improbable collection of women (including a couple of transsexuals).

> *L'Auberge Espagnole* (The Spanish Apartment), Cédric Klapisch (2002) – A young Parisian from the suburbs, Xavier, goes to Barcelona to learn Spanish for business. It ain't easy when university classes are given half the time in Catalan, but Xavier has no yen to return to Paris.

> *El Gran Gato,* Ventura Pons (2003) – A kind of musical dedicated to the singer-songwriter Javier Patricio 'Gato' Pérez.

> *Gaudí Afternoon,* Susan Seidelman (2001) – Judy Davis portrays a translator living in Barcelona in this flick about an American woman, Frankie, who asks Cassandra (played by Davis) to help her search for her husband, who has run away with their daughter and his lover.

> *Barcelona,* Whit Stillman (1994) – Two American cousins get tangled up in Barcelona, where love, politics and a little terrorism are the ingredients of this so-so film with some striking views of the city.

The most visible development has been on the northeast stretch of the coast, now home to the Parc del Fòrum (p98) and the surrounding Diagonal Mar residential district.

ART

Northern Catalonia is sprinkled with hundreds of early medieval stone churches and chapels. They were once spectacularly filled with bright Romanesque frescoes that served as didactic material for the mostly illiterate faithful. Today, a grand collection of the best of these frescoes can be seen in Barcelona in the Museu Nacional d'Art de Catalunya (MNAC; p148).

Painters of the Romanesque and early Gothic periods were largely anonymous but later some bright lights began to emerge and sign their works, almost always of a religious nature. Ferrer Bassá (c 1290–1348) was one of the region's first recognised masters. Influenced by the Italian school of Siena, his few surviving works include murals with a slight touch of caricature in the Monestir de Pedralbes (p135).

Bernat Martorell (1400–52), a master of chiaroscuro who was active in the mid-15th century, was one of the region's leading exponents of International Gothic, while Jaume Huguet (1415–92) adopted the sombre realism of the Flemish school, lightening the style with Hispanic splashes of gold.

Not until the late 19th century did artists of note again emerge in Catalonia. Led by dandy Ramon Casas (1866–1932) and his pal Santiago Rusiñol (1861–1931), the Modernistas were for a while the talk of the town. At the same time, Málaga-born Pablo Picasso (1881–1973) spent his formative adolescent years in Barcelona, where he created the paintings of his Blue Period. He moved to Paris in 1904, went on to experiment with Cubism and become one of the greatest artists of the 20th century. Continuing the burst of brilliance was the Barcelona-born surrealist Joan Miró (1893–1983), best remembered for his use of symbolic figures in primary colours.

Antoni Tàpies (1923–), whose hallmark is the use of anything from sand to bits of furniture in his grand works, remains Barcelona's senior contemporary artistic icon today. Barcelona-born Jaume Plensa (1955–) is possibly Spain's best contemporary sculptor.

DIRECTORY

TRANSPORT

ARRIVAL & DEPARTURE

AIR

Most flights arrive at **Aeroport del Prat – Barcelona** (☎ 902 404704), 12km southwest of the city centre. Some low-cost airlines, including Ryanair, use Girona airport, 80km north of Barcelona.

Aeroport del Prat – Barcelona

Bus

The **A1 Aerobús** (☎ 93 415 60 20) runs from the airport to Plaça de Catalunya (€3.60; 30 to 40 minutes depending on traffic) via Plaça d'Espanya and Gran Via de les Corts Catalanes every eight to 10 minutes from 6am to midnight Monday to Friday (from 6.30am on weekends and holidays). Departures from Plaça de Catalunya are from 5.30am to 11.15pm Monday to Friday (6am to 11.30pm on weekends and holidays) and go via Estació Sants and Plaça d'Espanya. Buy tickets on the bus. A slower local bus, No 46, runs every half-hour to Plaça d'Espanya. You can use the T-10 multiride public transport ticket (see Travel Passes, opposite).

Train

Renfe's *rodalies* (local train) line 10 runs between the airport and Estació de França in Barcelona (about 35 minutes), stopping also at Estació Sants (the main train station) and central Passeig de Gràcia. Tickets cost €2.40, unless you have a T-10 multiride public transport ticket (see Travel Passes, opposite). The service from the airport starts at 6am.

Taxi

A ride to or from the centre, which takes about half an hour depending on traffic – costs €18 to €24. To book a taxi call ☎ 93 225 00 00, ☎ 93 300 11 00 or ☎ 93 303 30 33.

CLIMATE CHANGE & TRAVEL

Travel – especially air travel – is a significant contributor to global climate change. At Lonely Planet, we believe that all who travel have a responsibility to limit their personal impact. As a result, we have teamed with Rough Guides and other concerned industry partners to support Climate Care, which allows people to offset the greenhouse gases they are responsible for with contributions to energy-saving projects and other climate-friendly initiatives in the developing world. Lonely Planet offsets all staff and author travel.

For more information, turn to the responsible travel pages on www.lonelyplanet.com. For details on offsetting your carbon emissions and a carbon calculator, go to www.climatecare.org.

Girona-Costa Brava Airport

Bus Sagalés (☎ 902 361550; www.sagales.com) runs hourly services from Girona-Costa Brava airport to Girona's main bus and train station (€1.75, 25 minutes) in connection with flights. The same company runs direct Barcelona Bus services to/from Estació Nord bus station in Barcelona (one way/return €11/19, 70 minutes). A taxi to Barcelona would cost €120 or more.

GETTING AROUND

Barcelona has a user-friendly transport system. The efficient Metro stops close to most places of interest and is complemented by the suburban rail system, Ferrocarrils de la Generalitat de Catalunya (FGC), and an extensive bus network. In this book, the nearest Metro/bus/FGC stations or routes are noted after the M / bus / train symbols in each listing. The table over the page lists the best options for getting to some of the main areas of interest.

TRAVEL PASSES

Targetes are multiple-trip tickets that will save you time and money and are sold at most metro stations. T-10 (€6.65) gives you 10 trips on the Metro, buses and FGC trains. T-DIA (€5) gives unlimited travel on all transport for one day. Two-/three-/four-/five-day tickets for unlimited travel on all transport except *rodalles* cost €9.20/13.20/16.80/20.

> **TAKE THE TRAIN!**
>
> Direct overnight trains run to Barcelona from Milan, Paris and Zürich (for timetables, see www.renfe.es). Plenty of trains also connect Barcelona with Madrid. From London, take the **Eurostar** (www.eurostar.com) to Paris and change there. If you leave in the morning, you could have lunch and an afternoon's sightseeing or shopping in Paris before climbing aboard the Trenhotel at Paris Austerlitz at 8.32pm (arrival in Barcelona at 8.24am). You can book this trip at www.raileurope.co.uk. Otherwise, high-speed TGV trains run regularly from Paris to Montpellier, from where you can connect for direct services to Barcelona.

METRO & FGC

Transports Metropolitans de Barcelona (TMB; ☎ 010; www.tmb.net) runs a Metro system with six colour-coded lines. Single tickets, good for one journey, no matter how many changes you have to make, cost €1.20. The Metro operates from 5am to midnight Monday to Thursday, until 2am Friday and Saturday (and the day before public holidays), and 6am to midnight on Sunday.

The **FGC** (☎ 93 205 15 15; www.fgc.net) suburban rail network is handy for trips from Plaça de Catalunya to scattered attractions such as Tibidabo and Pedralbes. It operates on the same schedule as the Metro.

BUS

TMB buses (☎ 010; www.tmb.net) run between 6am and as late as 11pm (depending on the line) Monday to Thursday and until 2am Friday, Saturday and the days before holidays. Afterwards a reduced schedule of yellow *nitbusos* (night buses) operates until anything from 3am to 5am. Single tickets are €1.20.

TAXI

Taxis are reasonably priced and charges are posted inside passenger side windows. The trip from Estació Sants to Plaça de Catalunya, about 3km, costs around €8. You can call a **taxi** (☎ 93 225 00 00, 93 300 11 00, 93 303 30 33, 93 322 22 22) or flag one down in the streets. General information is available on ☎ 010.

TRAM

Of the four new **tram lines** (☎ 902 193275) only the one from behind the zoo near the Ciutadella-Vila Olímpica Metro stop to Sant Adrià via the Fòrum might be of interest. All standard transport tickets and passes are valid.

TRIXI

Three-wheeled **cycle taxis** (www.trixi.info) operate on and around the

Recommended Modes of Transport

	Park Güell	Passeig de Gràcia	La Sagrada Família
Park Güell	n/a	Metro + walk 20min	Metro + walk 30min
Passeig de Gràcia	Metro + walk 20min	n/a	Metro + walk 15min
La Sagrada Família	Metro + walk 30min	Metro + walk 15min	n/a
Montjuïc	funicular + Metro 40min	funicular + Metro 25-30min	funicular + Metro
La Barceloneta	Metro + bus + walk 45min	Metro + walk 25min	Metro + walk 30min
Tibidabo	funicular + bus + walk + Metro 55min	funicular + tram + Metro or bus 60-70min	funicular + tram + Metro
La Rambla	Metro + walk 25min	walk 5-10min	walk + Metro 20min

waterfront (noon to 8pm June to October). They can take two passengers and cost €10/18 per half-hour/hour.

PRACTICALITIES

BUSINESS HOURS

Folks in Barcelona work Monday to Friday from 8am or 9am to 2pm and then again from 4.30pm or 5pm for another three hours. Department stores open from 9am to 10pm Monday to Saturday; a growing number of shops skip the lunch break.

Banks tend to open from 8.30am to 2pm Monday to Friday. Some open again from around 4pm to 7pm on Thursday evenings and/or Saturday mornings from around 9am to 1pm. The **main post office** (Map pp76-7, D6; ☎ 902 197197; www.correos.es in Spanish; Plaça d'Antoni López) opens from 8.30am to 10pm Monday to Saturday and noon to 10pm on Sunday. Many other branches tend to open from 8.30am to 2.30pm Monday to Friday and 9.30am to 1pm on Saturday.

Restaurants open for lunch from around 1pm to 4pm and reopen for dinner from 8pm to midnight; locals wouldn't dream of eating before 2pm and 9.30pm respectively.

Montjuïc	La Barceloneta	Tibidabo	La Rambla
Metro + funicular 40min	bus + Metro + walk 45min	Metro + walk + bus + funicular 55min	walk + Metro 25min
Metro + funicular 25-30min	Metro + walk 25min	Metro + tram + funicular or bus 60-70min	walk 5-10min
Metro + funicular 25-30min	Metro + walk 30min	Metro + tram + funicular or bus 60-70min	Metro + walk 20min
n/a	funicular + Metro	funicular + Metro	funicular + Metro 20-25min
Metro + funicular 25-30min	n/a	Metro + tram + funicular or bus 70-80min	Metro + walk 25min
Metro + funicular 25-30min	funicular + tram + Metro	n/a	funicular + tram + Metro or bus 60-70min
Metro + funicular 20-25min	Metro + walk 25min	Metro + tram + funicular or bus 60-70min	n/a

DISCOUNTS

Articket (www.articketbcn.org) gives you admission to seven important art galleries, including the Museu Picasso and Museu Nacional d'Art de Catalunya (MNAC), for €20 and is valid for six months.

The **Barcelona Card** costs €23/28/31/34 (a little less for children aged four to 12) for two/three/four/five days and could be worthwhile if you intend to cram in a lot. You get free transport (and 20% off the Aerobús) and discounted admission (up to 30% off) or free entry to many sights. Both cards are available at tourist offices.

The Ruta del Modernisme pack is well worth looking into. See the Neighbourhoods chapter (p107).

HOLIDAYS

New Year's Day 1 January
Epiphany 6 January
Good Friday Late March/April
Easter Monday Late Mar/April
Labour Day 1 May
Dilluns de Pasqua Grande (day after Pentecost Sunday) May/June
Feast of St John the Baptist 24 June
Feast of the Assumption 15 August
Catalonia's national day 11 September
Festes de la Mercè (five-day festival for co-patron saint Nostra Senyora de la Mercè) 24 September
Spain's National Day 12 October
Constitution Day 6 December
Feast of the Immaculate Conception 8 December
Christmas Day 25 December
St Stephen's Day (Boxing Day) 26 December

INTERNET

Internet centres abound in Barcelona. A growing number of hotels offer wi-fi access and/or high-speed modem access in rooms. A paying wi-fi service operates at the airport and train stations. Some cafés (such as Starbucks) also offer pay-as-you-go wi-fi connections.

Certain internet centres offer student rates and also sell cards for several hours' use at reduced rates. Following is a handful of options:

Bornet (Map pp76-7, D4; ☎ 93 268 15 07; www.bornet-bcn.com; Carrer Barra de Ferro 3; per 1/5hr €2.60/10; 10am-10pm Mon-Fri, 3-10pm Sat & Sun; M Jaume I)

easyInternetcafé (Map p65, B1; ☎ 93 412 13 97; www.easyeverything.com; Ronda de l'Universitat 35; per hr, depending on demand, around €1.70; 8am-2am; M Universitat). There is another branch on La Rambla (Map p47, B5; ☎ 93 318 24 35; La Rambla 31; 8am-2.30am; M Liceu)

Internet MSN (Map p127, C4; Carrer del Penedès 1; per hr €1.20; 9.30am-2am; M Fontana)

Some useful websites:

Ajuntament de Barcelona (Barcelona Town Hall; www.bcn.es) Has numerous links of general and tourist interest.

Barcelona.com (www.barcelona.com) A general tourist information site with many links.

Barcelona On-Line (www.barcelona-on-line.es) Similar to Barcelona.com.

Barcelona Reporter (www.barcelonareporter.com) An English-language site with news reports on Barcelona and Catalonia.
Barcelona Turisme (www.barcelonaturisme.com) The city's extensive tourist-office site.
BCN Nightlife (www.bcn-nightlife.com) A reasonable nightlife listings site.
Lecool (www.lecool.com) A free subscription site to what's on in Barcelona now.
Ruta del Modernisme (www.rutadelmodernisme.com) A specific site on Modernisme in Barcelona.

LANGUAGE

Barcelona is a bilingual city, with all locals speaking Catalan and Spanish. Many Spaniards who have moved here from elsewhere tend to speak Spanish only. A growing number of people speak at least some English. No-one expects you to learn any Catalan, but a few words of Spanish can go a long way. Where necessary, the masculine and feminine endings (usually 'o' and 'a' respectively) for words and phrases are given here.

BASICS

Hello.	*¡Hola!*
Goodbye.	*¡Adiós!*
Yes.	*Sí.*
No.	*No.*
Please.	*Por favor.*
Thank you.	*Gracias.*
You're welcome.	*De nada.*
Excuse me.	*Perdón.*
Sorry/ Excuse me	*Lo siento/ Discúlpeme.*

Do you speak English?
¿Habla inglés?
I don't understand.
No entiendo.
How much is this?
¿Cuánto cuesta esto?
Where are the toilets?
¿Dónde están los servicios?

GETTING AROUND

Where is the metro station?
¿Dónde está la parada de metro?
I want to go to…
Quiero ir a…
Can you show me (on the map)?
¿Me puede indicar (en el plano)?
When does the…leave/arrive?
¿A qué hora sale/llega el…?

bus	*autobús/bus*
Metro	*metro*
train	*tren*

AROUND TOWN

I'm looking for…
Estoy buscando…

a bank	*un banco*
the cathedral	*la catedral*
the hospital	*el hospital*
the police	*la policía*

EATING

breakfast	*desayuno*
lunch	*comida*
dinner	*cena*

I'd like the set menu.
Quisiera el menú del día.
I'm a vegetarian.
Soy vegetariano/a.

TIME, DAYS & NUMBERS

What time is it?	*¿Qué hora es?*
today	*hoy*
tomorrow	*mañana*
yesterday	*ayer*
morning	*mañana*
afternoon	*tarde*
evening	*noche*
Monday	*lunes*
Tuesday	*martes*
Wednesday	*miércoles*
Thursday	*jueves*
Friday	*viernes*
Saturday	*sábado*
Sunday	*domingo*
0	*cero*
1	*uno/una*
2	*dos*
3	*tres*
4	*cuatro*
5	*cinco*
6	*seis*
7	*siete*
8	*ocho*
9	*nueve*
10	*diez*
100	*cien/ciento*
1000	*mil*

EMERGENCIES

Help!	*¡Socorro!*
Call a doctor!	*¡Llame a un médico!*
Call the police!	*¡Llame a la policía!*
I'm lost.	*Me he perdido/a.*

MONEY

CURRENCY

Spain's currency is the euro. **Interchange** (Map p47, B4; ☎ 93 342 73 11; La Rambla dels Caputxins 74; 🕑 9am-midnight Apr-Sep, 9am-9pm Mon-Fri, to 2pm Sat Oct-Mar; Ⓜ Liceu) is centrally located and represents American Express.

COSTS

Locals complain that prices (but not wages) are rapidly approaching those of other major European centres. That is not entirely true. Cocktails can easily cost €6 to €8 nowadays, but a set lunch can still be had for under €10. Public transport and taxis remain cheaper than just about anywhere else in Europe. Many museums have free admission days.

NEWSPAPERS & MAGAZINES

The national *El País*, slightly left of centre, includes a daily supplement devoted to Catalonia. *La Vanguardia* (with a good listings magazine on Friday) and *El Periódico* are the main local Castilian-language dailies. The conservative and Catalan nationalist–oriented daily, in Catalan, is *Avui*. The Catalan daily *El Punt* concentrates on news in and around Barcelona. A plethora of international press is available at main central city newsstands, especially along La Rambla.

The city's tourist board publishes *Barcelona – The Official Gay and Lesbian Tourist Guide* bi-annually. A couple of informative free magazines are in circulation in gay bookshops and bars. One is the biweekly *Shan-guide*, jammed with listings and contact ads. The monthly *MENsual* (€2) is available at newsstands.

ORGANISED TOURS

The **Oficina d'Informació de Turisme de Barcelona** (Map p65, C2; ☎ 93 285 38 34; Plaça de Catalunya 17-S; Ⓜ Catalunya) organises guided walking tours that cover various areas of the city. Explore the Barri Gòtic; follow in Picasso's footsteps (including the Museu Picasso); observe the main jewels of Modernisme; and take in traditional purveyors of fine foodstuffs, from chocolate to sausages, across the Old City. All tours last 1½ to two hours and start at the tourist office, where you can find out the latest schedules. They cost €9 to €11 for adults and €3 to €5 for children.

TELEPHONE

Telefónica phonecards for payphones can be purchased in €6 and €12 denominations from tobacconists and post offices. Cut-rate phonecards for cheap international calls are also available from many tobacconists and some newsstands.

MOBILE PHONES

Spain uses the GSM cellular phone system, compatible with phones sold across the rest of Europe, and in Australia and most of Asia, but not those from North America and Japan (unless you have a tri band handset). Check with your service provider that it has a roaming agreement with a local counterpart, which can be expensive. You are able to buy pay-as-you-go SIM cards from local providers for approximately €10, which are useful, but only provided your phone is unblocked.

COUNTRY & CITY CODES

The city code (including the leading 9) is an integral part of the number and must always be dialled, whether calling from next door or abroad. The codes are as follows:

Spain ☎ 34
Barcelona ☎ 93

USEFUL NUMBERS

International access code ☎ 00
International directory inquiries ☎ 11825
International operator & reverse charges (collect)
Europe ☎ 1008
rest of the world ☎ 1005
Local directory inquiries ☎ 11818

TIPPING

You aren't expected to tip on top of restaurant service charges, but it is common to leave a small amount, say €1 per person. If there is no service charge, a 10% tip is optional. In bars, locals often leave small change (€0.05 to €0.10). Tipping taxi drivers is not common practice, but you should tip the porter (€1 to €2) at higher-class hotels.

TOURIST INFORMATION

In addition to the following tourist offices, several information booths operate at least through the summer.

Oficina d'Informació de Turisme de Barcelona (Map p65, C2; ☎ 93 285 38 34; www.barcelonaturisme.com; Plaça de Catalunya 17-S, underground; ⏲ 9am-9pm; Ⓜ Catalunya) The main Barcelona tourist information office. There are branches in the Barri Gòtic (Map p47, C3; ⏲ 9am-8pm Mon-Fri, 10am-8pm Sat, 10am-2pm Sun & holidays; Ⓜ Jaume I); Estació Sants (Map pp144-5, B1; ⏲ 8am-8pm Jun-Sep, 8am-8pm Mon-Fri, to 2pm Sat, Sun & holidays Oct-May; Ⓜ Sants Estació); and El Prat airport Terminal B arrivals hall (⏲ 9am-9pm).

Palau Robert regional tourist office (Map p127, D6; ☎ 93 238 40 00; www.gencat.net/probert; Passeig de Gràcia 107; ⏲ 10am-7pm Mon-Sat, to 2pm Sun; Ⓜ Diagonal)

Palau de la Virreina arts information office (Map p47, A3; ☎ 93 301 77 75; La Rambla de Sant Josep 99; ⏲ 10am-8pm Mon-Sat, 11am-3pm Sun; Ⓜ Liceu) A useful office for events information and tickets.

TRAVELLERS WITH DISABILITIES

Some hotels, monuments and public institutions have wheelchair access. All Metro stations should be wheelchair adapted (with lifts) by 2008. Buses already are. Many road crossings have been made wheelchair friendly in recent years. Crossing lights are adapted for the sight-impaired.

Accessible Barcelona (☎ 93 446 23 03; www.accessiblebarcelona.com) is run by Craig Grimes, a T6 paraplegic and inveterate traveller. Hotels are well researched and the company will help with transport and other aspects of your trip.

>INDEX

See also separate indexes for See (p203), Shop (p205), Eat (p206), Drink (p207) and Play (p208).

000 map pages

000 map pages

000 map pages

000 map pages

INDEX

SEE

EAT

000 map pages

PLAY

000 map pages